Walking Through the Storm

By

Cynthia Wester

authorHOUSE™

1663 LIBERTY DRIVE, SUITE 200
BLOOMINGTON, INDIANA 47403
(800) 839-8640
WWW.AUTHORHOUSE.COM

First published by AuthorHouse 2/21/2006

ISBN: 1-4208-1228-9 (sc)

Library of Congress Control Number: 2004098778

Printed in the United States of America
Bloomington, Indiana

This book is printed on acid-free paper.

Table of Contents

Acknowledgements ix

Introduction xi

Chapter One There's A Storm Coming 1

Chapter Two The Storm Arrives 13

Chapter Three The Storm Intensifies 31

Chapter Four God's Presence In The Storm 47

Chapter Five God's Care 67

Chapter Six God Calms The Storm 81

Chapter Seven The Storm Loses Its Intensity 101

Chapter Eight The Storm Is Over 117

Chapter Nine Lessons Learned From The Storm ... 135

Chapter Ten New Life Springs Forth 143

Bibliography 159

Dedication: In Loving Memory Of My Grandson

Bryson Allen Wester

Acknowledgements

No book can be written without the support of many. This book is no exception. I thank the Lord for the loving support of my wonderful husband, Stanley, our beautiful children son, Adam, our daughter, Kimberly, and husband, Jeffrey Allen Riddle, our precious grandchildren, LeMarqus Jayce Wester, Kamryn Alynne Riddle, and Jeffrey Allen Riddle Jr., and the encouragement of a host of friends and the prayers of many.

I would like to give a special thanks to Mary Alice Douglass and Le Nora Moore for their assistance in bringing this book to print.

Introduction

Storms are fascinating; some are quite dangerous to human life. There are various types of storms. To name a few, there are, Thunder, Cyclones, Monsoons, Hurricanes, Wind, Sand, Dust, Tornadoes, Tropical, etc.

All of mankind is subjected at one time or another, to the storms of life. To the Christian, this begins the marvelous walk of faith, with the sovereign God of the Holy Bible. Some storms can be seen at a distance, while others, erupt suddenly and without warning into our lives, with an abruptness that is startling.

It was during the personal storm in the lives of our son and his family, revolving around the sudden death of their six-month old son Bryson that we all felt a tremendous storm brewing. It was in this storm that our son and his family came under the close scrutiny of the Police, Media, and the Department of Children Services. Needless, to say, the ensuing days were difficult, but true to His word, the Lord, "never left us, or forsook us," and He brought us though.

As a result of this specific storm, this book was born. It was written to provide hope to all those who must walk through the storms of life.

Chapter One
There's A Storm Coming

Have you ever looked up in the sky and seen a storm coming? Most of us, learn to read the sky at a fairly young age, for signs of an approaching storm. One of the signs of a storm formulating on the horizon, is the formation of dark clouds on what might, otherwise be a clear and sunny day. Another good indication that a storm is brewing, can be the clap of thunder booming off in the distance, or lightning dancing its way across the sky.

There are some storms that actually take us by surprise. The day might be sunny, and suddenly, without warning, a rain shower pelts the earth with such intensity that it leaves no question in anyone's mind how quickly a storm might arise and seemingly out of nowhere. This makes the element of surprise very effective.

Life produces storms as well. Some you can see coming, while others you don't. How you handle the storm is very important. The types of storms addressed in this book will be both natural and spiritual.

I have experienced a number of storms in my own life. I too, have watched from a safe distance, and with interest, approaching storms both in the natural and spiritual realms. I have also observed that some storms are short in duration, while others create such havoc in our lives, that the devastation can be felt for years. Simply put, when a storm cloud burst into my life, I immediately rush into the presence of my Savior. As a believer and a child of God, I have a secure relationship with God, who is my heavenly Father. This enables me to place my faith in a God who promises, "never to leave or forsake me." This same child-like faith helps me to put life in its proper perspective. Jesus stipulated that all "those who are weary and heavy laden, come unto Him and He would provide rest for their soul." Mark 11:28. A number of life's storms are so overwhelming that there is no way that we can weather them on our own.

In both the natural and spiritual realms, when we realize that a storm may soon invade **our** space, we might experience a certain amount of uncertainty and/ or trepidation. Ask anyone who lives along costal areas, how they feel when faced with "storm after storm," how they feel when additional storms are predicted making their presence known in the region. Most inhabitants along costal shores begin preparations, and then attempt to wait it out. Most people begin their preparations by boarding up and securing their houses and businesses. They wisely store up food and in areas where the tide might have a tendency to rise, they might pile up sand bags, which will provide additional protection against the rising water that will gush into the area. Even with all necessary preparations in place, their attempt to protect themselves from the storm might prove to be futile. The onslaught of the storm might prove too severe, and a massive evacuation of the area, must take place to provide the safety needed from the ferociousness of the storm. In preparation for the writing of this book, I read scientific data gathered by the experts. A few facts emerge that have made this study interesting.

Let it be noted: "Man lives at the bottom of a dense and turbulent sea of gases." "The mixture of Nitrogen, Oxygen, Argon, and Carbon Dioxide, collectively known as air, can be subjected to tremendous currents; swirling and flowing at different speeds, pressures, and temperatures. A single thunderstorm can release 125 million gallons of water and discharge enough heat to supply the entire United States with electrical power for twenty minutes."[1]

In the gospel according to Mark, Jesus said to His disciples, "let us cross over to the other side." As the narrative continues, we see Jesus and His disciples leaving the multitude of people, that He had been teaching, They began to travel by boat to the other side of the shore. Suddenly and without warning a great gust of wind arose on the calm sea, and the boat began to sway violently, as harsh waves beat against its sides. The disciples became afraid; even though some were seasoned sailors. The storm threatened their safety

---

[1]   Whipple, A.B.C. and the Editors, "Planet Earth – Storm": Time Life Books. Page 6

and disrupted their peace of mind. In their anxiety, the disciples woke Jesus and with much fear, they asked Him, "Teacher, do you not care that we are perishing?" Jesus arose, rebuked the wind and said to the sea, **"Peace Be Still."** The wind ceased and there was calm on the sea; He said to them, **"Why are you so fearful?"** **"How is it that you have no faith?"** The gospel writer said, that this only made them more afraid; and they said among themselves, Who can this be, that even the Wind and Sea obey Him? Mark 4:37-41.

We have already noted that the Human Race can be exposed to such elements as Tornadoes, Cyclones, Hurricanes, Ice Wind, Dust, Sand, Tropical and Thunder Storms, and the like. These storms can create such havoc in our lives both emotionally and financially that the damage can take a toll on human life and cause poverty for many years to come.

If I have learned anything, it is that you can't stop the storms from coming. Later, we might surmise that there was something overlooked in our preparations, or we failed to take unto account the one thing that could have averted the storm. Nonetheless, the storm still arrived in spite of our highest level of preparations.

When September 11, 2001, arrived, we were for the most part, a nation totally unprepared for that day's horrific events.

Months later, the F.B.I., C.I.A., and other "Intelligence," sources of our great nation, were found accusing one another of "dropping the ball," by not providing enough data, that could have stopped or at least, counter-acted such an attack. "Intelligence sources," tell us that even if we had picked up on the fact that "something" was about to happen, specifics were not forthcoming. Hence, we experienced the element of surprise. So many questions arise after a national tragedy has transpired, therefore evoking emotions of confusion, grief, loss, anger, and desperation, just to name a few. Statements often emerge such as, "if only we had known, we would have been better prepared," or our "homeland security, could have provided protection to our citizens and prevented the bombings of the Pentagon and World Trade Centers." Some contend that if their loved ones would have stayed home from work on that tragic day; thus they would have been alive today. Who knows if things would have been any different? Granted, some things, we might have done differently, such as not going to work, if you worked at the Pentagon or one of the World Trade Centers, or even responded with a counter-attack issued through the channels of Homeland Security. What would our preparations have been if we had only known what was to take place on that tragic day? Again, we say even our best efforts could not have prevented the storm from arriving.

Often we wonder when tragedies arise "Where is God?" or "How can God, who is a God of Love, allow bad things to happen?" Make no mistake about it; God is a God of Love:

"For God so loved the world that
He gave His only begotten Son,
that whoever believes in Him
should not perish, but have
everlasting life."

John 3:16

Scripture records that the source of all our troubles is Satan. In his rebellion against God, he was kicked out of heaven, taking a third of the angelic host with him that were equally as rebellious. Thus, this descent to the earth, put the earth under the curse of sin and death; because of Adam and Eve's sin, we now live in a fallen world.

Satan (the devil) and a hosts of demons have tricked, and brought pain and suffering, to the sons of men.

In Isaiah 14:12-15, describes Satan's downfall: "How" you are fallen from Heaven; Oh Lucifer, "Son of the Morning!" "How you are cut down to the ground, you have weakened the nations;" Yet you shall be brought down to Sheol, to the lowest depths of the Pit."

Look at how Satan, in his pride and rebellion, dared to challenge the Most High God of all creation. Note what the Prophet Isaiah describes Satan as boasting what he would do to be above God, and to be worshipped as God.

1. I WILL ascend into Heaven;
2. I WILL exalt my throne above the stars of God;
3. I WILL also sit on the mount of the congregation, on the farthest side of the North;

4. I WILL ascend above the heights of the clouds;

5. I WILL be like the Most High."

This bold, and audacious creature, wanted to be God, and his agenda has never changed his desire to be worshipped as God. This is why God hates pride, whether from a tyrant over a nation, or in the individual heart; it alienates us from Him.

In the garden, Adam and Eve were separated by sin from fellowship with God. That old serpent (the devil) enticed Eve into sin, and Adam made a willing choice to do the same. After they were created by God, being made in the express image of God, they were told they could partake of every tree in the garden, except the tree of the "Knowledge of Good and Evil, for in the day, you shall eat of it, you shall surely die." Genesis 2:17.

Once they sinned, they became aware that they were naked, and they fashioned fig leaves to hide their nakedness. In the cool of the day, God made his presence known in the garden, but Adam and Eve ran and hid themselves among the trees. God called unto Adam, **"Where are you?"** Adam responded, "When I heard your voice, I was afraid, because I was naked." **"Who told you that you were naked?"** God said, **"Have you eaten from the tree that I commanded you not to eat?"** Adam, shifting the blame, said "the woman that you gave to be with me, she gave me of the tree, and I ate!" Then God turned His piercing gaze upon Eve, and the Lord God said to the woman, **"What is this you have done?"** The woman said, the serpent deceived me, and I ate!"

Let us clearly understand, that sin carries the consequences of death, both physically and spiritually. When sin entered the garden, Adam and Eve placed the entire human race under the penalty of death, and warranted separation from God. It was not until Jesus Christ (often referred to as the second Adam), by His own sacrificial death on the cross, the penalty of man's sin could be absolved.

There are two passages of scripture that say it best: "He was wounded for our transgressions, He was bruised for our iniquities (sins), the chastisement for our peace was upon Him, and by His stripes we were healed." All we like sheep have gone astray; we have turned every one to His own way, and the Lord has laid on Him the iniquity of us all." Isaiah 53:5-6.

1 Corinthians 5:21 says, "For He (God) made Him (Jesus) who knew no sin to be sin for us, that we might become the righteousness of God in Him."

In the Gospel according to John, we learn that the "Word (Jesus) became flesh and dwelt among us, and we beheld His glory as of, the only begotten of the Father, full of grace and truth." John 1:14.

John also tells us that, "In the beginning was the Word and the Word was God." John 1:1. This proves Jesus' claim of divinity, He was God, and He existed with God, the Father, from the beginning.

In East Tennessee, from time to time, we experience Ice Storms, needless, to say that can prove to be a detriment to road travel. Black Ice is even more hazardous to travel, since it isn't as easily visible to the naked eye.

It has already been stipulated, that we cannot prevent the arrival of storms. A good analogy, would be running out to stop the approaching storm with our bare hands, while the thunder claps, the wind howls and increases its intensity, and soon the storm erupts, and you are forced to run for cover.

Chapter Two
The Storm Arrives

Anticipation of a storm's arrival can sometimes be far worse, than the arrival of the storm itself.

When a nation experiences a storm everyone is affected. In March 2003, our nation went to war with Iraq. Our objectives were, (1) to liberate the citizenry of Iraq, an oppressed people living under the evil regime of Saddam Hussein, and, (2) to keep from the hands of terrorist, weapons of mass destruction.

Weeks prior to the arrival of the war, we were forced to play the "waiting game." Initially, we had to wait to see if the United Nations Inspectors would discover weapons that violated U. N. resolutions and policies. Again, we waited to see if Saddam Hussein would comply with the adopted resolutions within a specified deadline. Meanwhile France, Germany, and Russia exerted pressure on the Security Council to coerce the United States to extend the deadline. When it became obvious that Saddam Hussein would defiantly disregard all deadlines, President George Bush, gave the order that sent the troops into battle. Indeed the storm had arrived!

War is never easy. Even after the first bomb was dropped, protest could be heard in our country as well as around the world. The cries for "peace," grew louder, as many became disillusioned with the Bush Administration. Deployment of the troops continued into the region. The coalition of British and American troops swarmed into the deserts of Kuwait, where they faced blinding dust and sand storms propelled by fierce winds.

The waiting game continued, as troops waited to see when they would be able to begin the three mile trek, inch by inch, into Baghdad; where the first bombs and air strikes of the war would begin.

Not everyone agrees that a nation should go to war in what seems like "peace times." However, let it be noted that whether you agree or disagree, once the command to strike is given by the Commander In-Chief, support of our troops and their families is imperative. Remember it is for the "freedom of speech," and other liberties that so many brave men and women have fought for, and will continue to fight for, in the future of our great nation.

Several questions might arise when we seek to get God's take on warfare. In order to fully comprehend, or best understand God's perspective, we would need to look at God's chosen nation, the Israelites.

The Old Testament writers, recorded the Israelites, as living in close proximity to their enemies. When Israel depended on the Lord her God, she was victorious, in overcoming the enemy. When they sought to win by their own human efforts, they often lost the battle, or sustained great loss of life.

In the book of Judges, we see that the children of Israel did evil in the sight of the Lord, and He delivered them into the hands of the Midianites, Amalekites, and the people East of them, for seven years. It was under the siege of the Midianites, that the Israelites became an oppressed and impoverished people.

It wasn't long before Israel's enemies sought to enter their land to destroy it.

Gideon, a young farmer, was given the task of delivering the Israelites from the Midianites and Amalekites; Gideon received word from the Lord, that He would be with him in battle against the Midianites and the great company up against Israel, to do battle with them. The Lord promised to help them defeat the enemy by delivering them into their hands. Gideon took great comfort in these words, but he wanted to be sure that the victory would be theirs, so he put God to the test by putting out a fleece.

When God demonstrated His power, Gideon was reassured that God was with him. Gideon gathered a great number of people with him to do battle.

Again, the word of the Lord came, **"that there are too many people with you."** Gideon was instructed to reduce the number by asking, "whoever is afraid, you may return home;" and the number was reduced from twenty-two thousand to ten-thousand.

God told Gideon that there are still too many, and to test them, and those who drank from the water in a specific fashion were to go with Gideon into battle, and the number of them was reduced to three hundred.

Then God gave Gideon further instructions. They were to enter the camp of the Midianites at night, armed only with their trumpets, and their pitchers in their hands, and once again, God reassured Gideon, He had delivered the Midianites into his (Gideon's) hands.

Can you just imagine how Gideon must have felt, given such strange instructions? He probably felt that the task at hand was a bit overwhelming. Not only did they not have proper weapons, but the number of three hundred men seemed grossly inadequate to come up against, (so large an army), and win the battle. Let's interject at this point to say, sometimes God gives the strangest instructions, but it is imperative that we obey them even if it seems to make no sense to us whatsoever. As this fascinating narrative goes, Gideon did as he was instructed.

As night fell, once inside the camp of the enemy, all three hundred surrounded the camp, every man standing quietly at attention in his assigned location.

Then they begin to blow their trumpets, brake their pitchers in their hands, while simultaneously shouting, "the sword of the Lord, and Gideon."

Then the army of the Midianites fled in fear, not realizing that only three hundred men had defeated them.

The battle was won by Israel's Jehovah Nissi, (The Lord Our Banner), who is mighty in battle. There is nothing impossible for the Lord our God. All glory and praise belonged to God alone. Read the account of this story in the book of Judges, Chapters 6 & 7.

The physical aspects of war are obvious, but the spiritual aspects of warfare are not always so clearly defined.

Paul addressed the spiritual aspects of warfare in his letter to the Corinthians. Paul stated "though we walk in the flesh, we do not war according to the flesh," "For the weapons of our warfare are not carnal, but mighty in God for the pulling down of strongholds." II Corinthians 10:3-5.

In order to best comprehend what Paul is saying, we must define the word stronghold. A "stronghold," is an enslavement of the spirit that keeps us from being free to walk in the spirit of God. The person who has a stronghold operative in his or her life, is a person who is in bondage, and who willingly believes the lies of the devil, rather than the truth of God's word.

Strongholds are satanic in nature, as previously stipulated, that can also ensnare a believer, who is not on guard. This is why Paul admonished the Ephesians, (Ephesians 6:11) to "put on the whole armor of God, that you might be able to stand up against the wiles (tricks) of the devil.

Examples of strongholds are: addictions, unforgiveness, and extreme despair over a loss. It is anything that exalts itself in our minds as being real, while pretending to be stronger than the power of God and His ability to deliver us from it.

When a person accepts Jesus Christ as Savior, that individual becomes a "new creature." That person is saved from hell's fire (eternal damnation), having been bought with the price of Jesus Christ's blood, they are moved from the kingdom of darkness to the kingdom of light.

Never again, do we have to worry about our salvation or whether we will go to heaven when we die. This has been accomplished through the death, burial, and resurrection of our dear Savior, the Lord Jesus Christ.

Even though the believer, now has a new nature, this nature many times wars with the old nature, and if not careful, the believer can fall into sin. How can this be you might ask? Since we live in a fallen world, under the influence of Satan, we can be enticed to sin.

The good news is that now being a new creature, we have the Holy Spirit of our Heavenly Father living within us, and convicting us of sin. "If we confess our sins, He is faithful to forgive us our sins, and to cleanse us from all unrighteousness. I John 1:9. Now we can be restored to a right relationship (fellowship) with our God.

Our position in Christ Jesus is secure. Because of our position, we have been made perfect through the death, burial, and resurrection of the Lord Jesus Christ.

Since we live in a fallen world under the curse of sin, we must die daily to our flesh (self). It is on a daily basis, that we must struggle with our, weaknesses of the flesh, faults, and those strongholds that so easily ensnare us in bondage. Has, He not told us in His word, "that without Me, you can do nothing?" the struggle intensifies when we attempt to live the Christian life in our own strength.

There are all kinds of spiritual storms that we, as believers, will encounter in this life. To name a few: sickness, sorrow, death, financial reversals, separation and divorce, betrayal in relationships, abuse (verbal, physical, sexual), gossip, jealousy, hatred, and murder, and the list goes on.

There are many storms in the natural that we encounter; the believer must encounter numerous spiritual storms as well. There are many afflictions (trials), in this life, but He who is faithful will deliver us from them all.

There are ways in which we can fight our spiritual battles:

1. Learn completely to look (depend) on the Lord for help; "Trust in the Lord with all your heart, and lean not to your own understanding; in all your ways acknowledge Him, and He shall direct your paths." Proverbs 3:5-6.

2. See God's power in the divine spiritual weapons that we have been given to fight our spiritual battles; daily the believer, "must put on the whole armor of God, to be fully armed and equipped (dressed for battle) to stand up against the fiery darts of the evil one." We must: (a) put on the breast plate of righteousness; (b) have our waist girded with truth; (c) slip into shoes that have the preparation of the gospel of peace; (d) take up the shield of faith, which will allow you to quench all the darts of the wicked one," and "take the helmet of salvation, and the sword of the spirit, which is the Word of God." Ephesians 6:11, No soldier goes into battle without being prepared.

3. Our weapons include knowledge of God's Word. We are to study God's Word, so that we are the type of workman that is not ashamed, rightly dividing (discerning) the Word of truth." II Timothy 2:15. In the next chapter, Paul tells Timothy that "all scripture is given by inspiration of God, and is profitable for doctrine, for reproof, for correction, for instruction in righteousness. II Timothy 3:16.

4. We must render our thoughts captive unto God. In the vain imaginations of our minds, we can place ourselves equal to God. We must learn to stand on the authority of God's Word. Satan has a field day in our minds, he can cause us to doubt God and doubt God's Word. Our thoughts can lead us away from God. Our fears can assail us to the point that we no longer trust the truth of God's Word.

We are to "trust in the Lord with all our heart, and lean not on our own understanding, in all our ways acknowledge Him, and He will direct our paths." Proverbs 3:5-6.

It has already been established that we as believers, now have at our disposal, spiritual weapons to fight the spiritual battles that we must encounter in this life. The Father, Son, and Holy Spirit, who resides within the heart of every believer, allows the believer to do just that.

John in I John 3:9, says that, "whosoever has been born of God, does not sin, for His seed remains in Him, and he cannot sin. Because he has been born of God.

Now, at first glance, we would think that this particular scripture to be contradictory, to what we already know; but a deeper study of this issue indicates that this is not the case.

Let's analyze what is being said. We have already established that we are capable of sinning even as believers. The case being, that as long as we live in these bodies, we are capable of succumbing to the flesh, and can fall into sin. "Our spirits are willing, but our flesh is weak." We will no longer be capable of sinning, only when we have transcended from the earthly realm, into the heavenly realm, through the vehicle of death.

One aspect of the believer's new nature is that now he or she has new desires. One such desire, in spite of struggles, is a desire to serve the Savior with their whole heart, keeping their lives as free from sin as possible. How do we live a life pleasing unto our Lord?

1.   By Learning to obey the Word of God, we should;
     a)   Allow the study of God's Word to manifest itself in and through your life;
     b)   Cry out to God from the temptations that would ensnare and cause you to do what is evil in His sight;
     c)   Pray that God will help you to live holy and righteously in His sight.

2. By asking God for His forgiveness of sin;
    a) Granting others that same forgiveness of sin for any offense rendered against you.
3. By seeking what is the perfect will of God.
4. By learning to express love to others, as God, has loved us;
    a) Witnessing to others the, "Gospel of Salvation," through faith in the Lord Jesus
    b) Loving others as Christ first loved you;
    c) Allowing God to receive the honor and glory in and through your life.

Basically what John is saying, in his first Epistle is, "that with Christ living within," we are no longer practitioners of sin (repeatedly ensnared by it. The Holy Spirit within "holds the reigns." daily "we must walk in the spirit, not to fulfill the lust of the flesh."

God has placed within mankind a spirit and a soul. God desires that we be whole in our bodies, spirits, minds and souls.

It is always interesting to observe how the human spirit is amazingly, resilient. Countless people have survived any number of human tragedies, from horrific accidents, chronic and terminal illnesses, disease, psychological maladies, murder of a loved one, and any number of human problems that tries the souls of men. The stresses of life, sometimes threatens to overwhelm the spirit. God invites us to cast our cares upon Him, because He cares for us." I Peter 5:7.

We must allow the holy spirit of God, who resides in the heart of every believer, to help us overcome our temptations and to triumph over our problems. There is no other way. We eventually have to admit, that we don't have the solutions to all of our problems; even when we undertake to solve our own problems, we often blow it!

Man may think of himself as being in control of world events, as well as his own personal circumstances, nothing is further from the truth. It is God who is in control of all things. It is He who "works His will," in the affairs of men. God is the Creator of the universe. All of creation is under the powerful and mighty hand of God. He is the Alpha (the beginning) and the Omega (the end). Revelation 1:8.

In the physical realm of storms, we must admit our helplessness when it comes to controlling the forces that govern the weather. There are times when a meteorologist can accurately predict the weather and its patterns and/or temperatures, but since the weather is under the control of God, we don't always hit it right on the mark.

In the spiritual realm of storms, we fare no better than in the physical. Spiritual storms can be storms that we were not expecting and must admit that we need God's help to stay-a-float, or we will go "down for the count."

Many of us are more excepting of the fact that we can not control the weather. However, it is more difficult for us to relinquish control of our life's circumstances to anyone other than ourselves, even God. We feel deep within, if we can be in control of life's difficulties, then circumstances will be more to our liking and we can manipulate these circumstances to where we feel most comfortable. Because of this human failing, we hate it when our lives spin out of control, and we don't know what to do, or we don't know what direction we must take to bring events back under our control. We want to know many times what the future holds. That's why so many consult psychics, rather than looking to God to bring us through the difficulties at hand.

God delights in our laying our cares upon Him. It is simply called trust. Our faith operates best, when we in total dependence upon God, allow Him to solve our problems. This proves to be beneficial for us, and gives us new strength in our walk with our God. We must learn to wait, (develop patience) for Him, as He works things out for our good.

How well the prophet Isaiah knew what it meant to wait upon the Lord his God. He said, "those who wait on the Lord, shall renew their strength; they shall mount up with wings, like eagles, they shall run and not be weary, they shall walk, and not faint." Isaiah 40:31. This verse has often brought me comfort. Reading it, I am aware, that even though my physical and spiritual strength is weak; I trust in my God to help me "run the race," with great confidence in my God's strength to see me through.

The troops in the deserts of Kuwait experienced the grit of the sand as it blew into all of the open cavities of their faces, often blinding them as well as frustrating their efforts to move forward to their destinations. They too, had to learn that they were under the control of the Almighty God.

Chapter Three
The Storm Intensifies

Every good cook knows that in food preparations, often the food must be cooked slowly, or even the heat turned down; then the mixture in the pot, is allowed to simmer for the best results. There are other times, when the heat must be turned up, and the intensity of the heat brings the results of a well-cooked meal

When we must go through great trial (severity of the storm), our vigilant Heavenly Father, watches the intensity of the heat. The fiery furnace experience often threatens our peace of mind, and we might feel like we can't go on or see our way through. Our tear-clouded eyes reveal the intensity of our pain, and we are tempted to give up hope as well as loose heart.

Many years ago when our oldest child, Kimberly, was just a toddler, we were returning home to Chicago, from Tennessee. Enroute to Chicago, by way of the expressway, we encountered weather conditions that turned into a raging snowstorm. By the time that we realized that weather conditions were worsening; there was no time to exit off the expressway. To make matters worse, we were in the middle of the highway, with very few cars around us, and with a frightened toddler. Needless to say, the situations had turned dangerous.

Silently, I began to pray, as my husband, Stanley, bravely navigated our course. We knew that we were in the hands of the Lord. God is always so very faithful, His presence was with us, and He brought us safely to our destination.

In May 2003, Tornadoes ripped through the plain states and the Southeastern part of the country. The hardest hit places were Pierce Missouri, Kansas City Missouri, Oklahoma and Jackson Tennessee. In the aftermath of the storms tornadoes, left plenty of property damages, and over 39 people were killed. It was estimated that over 235 tornadoes touched down.

In the intensity of the storm, video cameras recorded flying debris, overturned cars, and flattened buildings.

In many areas of East Tennessee, where I live, we experienced heavy rains, hail, and rising waters that led to flooding in quite a few areas across the region.

Two weeks prior to this, we were awaken at 5:00 a.m., by an earthquake, originating in, Alabama, shocks were felt through Georgia, Tennessee and into Kentucky. The quake registered 4.9 on the Richter Scale.

Intense storms, often called the "eye of the storm," teaches us to lean upon our Savior. Sometimes this can prove to be a difficult lesson for us to learn.

If anyone has ever felt intense heat it was the three Hebrew boys, literally placed in the fiery furnace. King Nebuchadnezzar, King of Babylon, had three young men among his captives, who refused to worship the, "image made of gold." These Jewish young men had been renamed while in captivity. They were renamed Shadrach, Meshach, and Abed-Nego. It wasn't long before it came to the attention of the King that these three young men refused to worship the golden image that he had set up. Taking this as an act of treason, the king ordered that the furnace be heated seven times hotter than usual, and that they be cast into the midst of the intense heat.

Shadrach, Meshach, and Abed-Nego, knew that under normal circumstances, there would be no way that they could survive the furnace's intense heat. Their faith was firmly placed in their God, the great God of Israel, He sees and answers prayers in the most difficult of circumstances. Under the king's most fierce command, the three were bound, and fully clothed, and taken to the furnace to be thrown in the depths of the furnace. The men who brought them to the furnace were immediately killed, by the heat.

When King Nebuchadnezzar looked into the burning furnace, the Scriptures tells us that he was, "astonished." The king turned to one of his counselors and said, "did we not cast three men, bound and fully clothed into the mist of the fire?" They answered, "it is true, oh king." "Look, he answered, I see four men loose, and walking in the midst of the fire, they are not hurt and the fourth one looks like the, "Son of God."

By refusing to bow down to a god, other than the true God of Israel, the three Israelites showed even a pagan king, that their God, awesome in power, is able to bring those who belong to Him through the most difficult circumstances. He is a God of deliverance.

It was apparent that they had not been singed by the flames or even smelled like smoke! What a great God we serve. He deserves all the glory and praise due Him. He is indeed "more than worthy to be praised." This King then declared that there is no God like the one that the Hebrew boys served. This story is recorded in Daniel, Chapter 3.

This is the same God that later spared Daniel in the Lion's Den, Daniel was a man of prayer, The Word of God tells us that at least three times a day, Daniel was found in the position of prayer; regardless of what was going on around Him. Needless to say, it must not have always been easy to pray, since he was a captive in a foreign land. Daniel had purposed in his heart, that he would not defile himself with the food from the king's table, the food that was offered to idols. Daniel resolutely determined in his heart, that he would not worship any false god, but his God, the true God.

Miracles have often happened because God's people have prayed. God's power has been displayed because people have prayed. God, has answered, and He will continue to answer, above our ability to ask and think"

To best understand the weapons of prayer, faith, and God's Word, let us explore more in-depth, these areas.

Prayer:

Prayer is communicating with God. We have been given access to God, through His son, the Lord Jesus Christ. We are encouraged to "pray without ceasing." I Thessalonians 5:17.

Even with a busy, hectic schedule, we can maintain an attitude of prayer, within our hearts. As believers, we are exhorted to "pray one for the other." Individuals united in prayer, touch the heart of God. Scripture teaches that our Heavenly Father, already knows what we need, even before we bring our petitions before Him in prayer, He wants us to ask Him for what we need. As we transverse along the avenue of prayer, we learn to pray in "accordance to His will, and He hears and answers our prayers.

God always answers our prayers; He answers with a yes, no, or wait. There is nothing that we can't bring to the Lord in prayer. There is nothing too trivial, or mundane that we can ask of Him in prayer, nor is there anything that we might ask, beyond His ability to handle.

In John 17th, He prayed for all believers, who were to come after Him. In Luke 11:1, He taught His disciples to pray (The Lord's Prayer).

No one knew better than King David, the source of his strength. At one point in his life before he became King, David literally ran from King Saul, who sought to take his life. Through other problems in his life, he often looked to God through prayer for help. The Psalmist poetically said:

I will lift up my eyes to the hills -
from whence comes my help?
My help comes from the Lord,
Who made heaven and earth. Psalms 121:1-2.

When troops were deployed into Iraq, we prayed as a nation, likewise we prayed for God to deliver the Pow's home safely and He did.

Satan, our adversary, does not want us to pray. He will do anything to discourage us from prayer, and he will do the same when we read God's word. We are "to resist him, by standing firm, and he will flee from us." James 4:7. Prayer is a powerful weapon against the lies of our enemy.

Sometimes people feel disappointed when God does not appear to answer prayer as they have prayed. Remember, that God has a perfect will for an individual's life, and He will do what is best for those who belong to Him. If we pray for healing for a person and they die, we should bow to the will of God. Total healing comes when a believer moves from the earthly realm to the spiritual realm. Total healing comes when a believer now resides in the presence of his or her Lord.

Prayer and faith, along with the word of God, is a force that no foe can over-power. Now let us examine the power of God's Word:

The Word of God:

The Bible is God's Word. It is a book like none other. In the Bible we come to learn that God loved us so very much, that while the world was under the weight of sin, God sent His only begotten son, who knew no sin, into the world to die for the sins of everyone. I John 5:11 say that "this testimony, that God has given us is eternal life, and this life is in His son."

"The Bible has sixty-six books, written by over forty authors. These authors were from every strata of society." "Some were renowned, and others were unknown." "Some were rich, while others were poor." "Some were Kings, others, were peasants. "Among the authors of the Scriptures were fishermen, scholars, politicians, philosophers, theologians, shepherds, farmers and rabbis." The sixty-six books were written in many places; deserts, mountains, prisons, palaces, islands and tents." "Some of the writings bring great joy, while others dismal despair." "The Bible was written in three languages, Hebrew, Aramaic and Greek, on three different continents, Europe, Asia, and Africa. The sixty-six books were written over sixteen hundred years ago."[2]

The Bible has been proven to be the infallible Word of God, relevant to the present and God's revelation of the future. It exhorts, comforts, and instructs us in

---

[2]   Morgan, Robert J. "Can Christianity Be Proven? Beyond Reasonable Doubt! Page 56

righteousness. It is our guidebook and manual for this our earthly journey.

The Bible contains the Gospel Message: The Good News of the Gospel is that Jesus, was born, died, buried, and resurrected according to the scriptures. It is the best news that I know.

"He is risen, as He said," the angel told the three women who, came to the garden early one Sunday morning. "Go and tell the disciples and Peter, that he is going before you into Galilee; there you will see Him as said to you." Mark 16:7.

The four synoptic gospels, Matthew, Mark, Luke and John, all give an account of these events, according to their own specific view points and eye witness reports.

In the book of Matthew: He is the Messiah; In Mark: He is the Wonder Worker; In the gospel according to Doctor Luke: He is the Son of God; and in John: He is the Son of Man. No other religion in the world can give documented proof of its leader being raised from the dead, other than Christianity.

Faith:

"Now Faith, is the substance of things hoped for, the evidence of things not seen;" "For by it the elders obtained a good report." (testimony) - "By faith we understand that the worlds were formed by the Word of God, so that the things which are seen were not made of things which are visible." Hebrews 11:1-3.

Hebrews, Chapter 11, is referred to as the "faith," chapter. This chapter gives an historical account of all those who have walked by faith. Often they were persecuted, nomads who often lived in caves, and dens. In some instances they lost their lives for their faith. Their faith sustained them, and enabled them to look toward a heavenly city, where the light of that city is the Lord Jesus.

Faith is a muscle that every believer must exercise in order to gain strength and experience the growth needed to "walk by faith."

In the middle of our spiritual storms, our faith can wane. In the middle of the storm, we can become discouraged, depressed and loose hope. This is why we must trust God's word, the truth of God's word, enables us to place our trust in Him, rather than our emotions.

We must ask God to give us the strength to continue to trust Him, when our storms look the darkest, or when the situations of life threaten to overwhelm us, and the circumstances look hopeless to us.

Paul always encouraged the early church not pray for deliverance from their afflictions, but that they learn to endure. He knew that they would be stronger in the faith, after they had gone through their trials, and received the victory that deliverance would bring. Scripture tells us "many are the afflictions of the righteous, but the Lord delivers us out of them all." II Corinthians 4:17, tells us that, "our light affliction, which is but for a moment, is working for us a far more exceeding and eternal weight of glory."

> There are times when we can experience more than one storm brewing at the same time. It is at this time that we must not give into despair, but depend solely on His strength. The prophet Isaiah says it best when he says, "but those who wait on the Lord, shall renew their strength; they shall mount up with wings like eagles, they shall run and not be weary, they shall walk and not faint" Isaiah 40:31.

Today, so many people put their trust solely in their education, social status, finances, material possessions, political clout, power, fortune, fame, and looks – now in themselves there is nothing wrong with achieving certain accomplishments, however, when we place them above God in our lives, they become an idol. On the altar of self-worship, we replace God with gods that cannot fill the void in our lives, that we are seeking, nor can they take the place of a vital, trusting and intimate relationship with the God, who has loved us with an everlasting love.

The salvation message of the cross, as depicted in the scriptures is simple. God loved us so much, that he sent His Son, who knew no sin, to pay the penalty of death for our sins. The Lord Jesus suffered a horrible death on the cross for you and me, and the entire human race. He shed His precious blood as atonement for sins; he became the sacrificial lamb when burnt offerings and animal sacrifices were no longer sufficient. God's son is the only way in which we can have eternal life. "This is the testimony that God has given us eternal life, and this life is in His son." I John 5:11

The death of God's Son is the only way that we can come to God and receive eternal life. We cannot work our way to heaven by doing good deeds. We cannot buy our way into heaven. We cannot talk our way in; Jesus said, **"I am the way, the truth, and the light, no man cometh to the Father except by me."**

There may be times when our faith might be small or doubts might assail us, remember that "without faith it is impossible to please God, for he who comes to God must believe that He is, and that He is a rewarded of all those who diligently seek Him.

Hebrews 11:6.

Summary:

Prayer is a powerful weapon that is needed to walk through the storms. We must never give up. Our break through might just be around the corner. God's grace is sufficient to sustain us through the darkest moments of our lives. "Men ought always to pray and not faint." Luke 18:1.

God's Word is God communicating with mankind. God's Word is a, "lamp to my feet, and a light to my path." Psalm 119:105. "Your word have I hidden in my heart; that I might not sin against you." Psalm

119:11. "The Word of God is living and powerful, and sharper than any two-edged sword, piercing even to the division of soul and spirit, and of joints and marrow, and is a discerner of the thoughts and intents of the heart." Hebrews 4:12.

When we trust God not only for our daily provisions and in every aspect of our lives, His power protects us from the intense heat of the storm. Our faith sustains us through every difficult situation that we must face. Our faith also sustains us even to the death of our physical bodies. "Let us hold fast the confession of our hope without wavering, for He who has promised is faithful." Hebrews 10:23.

Our weapons of Prayer, God's Word, and Faith are a strong defense against all of life's storms. They are even a strong defense against strongholds in our lives. Strongholds are detrimental to the believer.

How do you walk through, or wait out the storm, at its highest level of intensity? I know no other way, but to trust, pray, and stand firmly on the Word of God

Chapter Four
God's Presence In The Storm

Death has always been a mystery. We often go to funerals of family, friends, and loved ones; and in the back of our minds, we often wonder what it is like to leave this world in which we have lived.

Many people fear death; it is the fear of the unknown. We hear testimonies of individuals who claim they have had "after death experiences," but even their accounts do not totally satisfy our curiosity.

We are told that those who are saved enter into the presence of God their father. Basically we understand, that the grave holds the body of the deceased, which is subject to decay with the passing of time. The spirit and soul of man enters into either the presence of God the Creator of all life, or into a state of separation from God the Creator.

Paul in his letter to the to the Thessalonians addressed this subject. The Thessalonians wondered if they would ever see their loved ones again after they had passed from this life into the shadows of death.

Look at what he says in I Thessalonians 4:13-18. "We would not have you ignorant brethren concerning them that fall asleep (die), that you sorrow not as those who have no hope. We who are alive and remain until the coming of the Lord will by no means precede those who are asleep. For the Lord Himself will descend from heaven with a shout, with the voice of an archangel and with the trumpet of God, and the dead in Christ will arise first. Then we who are alive and remain shall be caught up together with them in the clouds to meet the Lord in the air, and thus we shall always be with the Lord." Paul suggested that they "comfort one another with these words." This event is known at the "Rapture of the Church." In Chapter 5, he reminds them to live soberly (seriously) for that day will come as a thief in the night (when no one expects it). Look at the words of Jesus: **"Watch therefore, for you know neither**

the day nor the hour, in which the Son of Man is coming." Matthew 25: 13 Jesus refers to Himself, coming for His bride, the church, coming as a thief in the night, all in a twinkling (blink) of the eye. Can you imagine being caught up to meet Him in the air as quickly as it takes to blink the eye? All those who are in their graves rise first, then believers who are alive, quickly follow.

Much attention in recent days has been given to the "Left Behind Series," co-authored by Dr. Tim LaHaye, popular theologian and author of "The Merciful God of Prophecy(a plan for the end times). In his compelling video, "The Rapture: Hope or Hoax, Dr. Jack Van Impe and wife Rexella, present proof that the Rapture will take place before the period called "The Tribulation." In his thirty tape series, "Triumph of the Lamb, Dr. Adrian Rogers of, Love Worth Finding, verifies biblical prophecy on the Rapture, Tribulation, and ensuing Judgments coming at the end of this age.

Critics scoff at those who believe in the Rapture. They accuse those who believe in the Rapture as having, "a pie-in-the sky mentality." Note that scoffers of the truth are nothing new; II Peter 3:3, gives credence to this fact. "Scoffers will come in the last days, walking according to their own lust, and saying: where is the promise of His coming? For since the fathers fell asleep, all things continue as they were from the beginning of creation. Beloved do not forget this one thing, that with the Lord, one day is as a thousand years, and a thousand years as one day. The Lord is not slack concerning His promise, as some count slackness, but is longsuffering toward us, not willing that any should perish, but that all should come to repentance."

Today we live in what can only be termed as "dangerous times." Our newspapers are full of crime. There are wars and rumors of wars. Many unsettling and strange occurrences of events play out in our world day by day. People are seeking peace, but seemingly there is very little on the earth. The world is turning to entertainment to help assuage the pain and struggles of this life. Only the one who knows Jesus as Savior can remain at peace in a chaotic world. The Bible foretold of these times. The Bible clearly states as time goes on, the condition of the world will only get worse. In order to understand biblical prophecy, and what happens in the end times, we must look into John's book of the

Revelation. We have already established that the next prophetic event to come is the Rapture of the Church. The Rapture of the Church heralds a new era in History. The Rapture signifies the close of, "The Church Age.," what happens next in the world will be the worse period of suffering that the world has ever known. There has never been a time like it, nor will there be, after its terrifying events have passed. This period of time is known as the "Great Tribulation."

Jesus did not want His servants ignorant about what would happen in the end times. The Apostle John was carried away in the spirit to a remote island, called Patmos, where he was instructed to write what would happen at the end of time. John penned in Revelation, Chapter 1, that he heard a loud voice loud as a trumpet say, **"I am the Alpha and the Omega, the First and the Last, and send it to the seven churches which are in Asia," "to Ephesus, to Smyrna, to Pergamos, to Thyatira. To Sardis, to Philadelphia, and to Laodicea."**

John wrote that plagues, and judgments would come upon the world such as the world has never seen before. To the reader, the book of the Revelation is not only symbolical, but literal as well. The terrible judgments will be literal and make our present day movie odysseys in science fiction look like a fairy tale. Imminent after the Rapture, the judgment of God falls upon the inhabitants of the earth. Revelation tells us that the judgment comes in the form of four riders called the horsemen of the Apocalypse. Revelation, Chapter 6. Each rider, on a specific color of horse, brings judgment to those on the earth; each judgment more terrifying and more deadly than its predecessor. Why is this going to happen, you might ask! Remember those that have accepted Jesus as Savior, and believed Him to be God, capable of saving them from their sins have been ruptured into His presence. The only ones left on the earth, are those who have refused God's offer of salvation through His Son, the Lord Jesus. They must now face the wrath of God on the "sons of disobedience."

Now let us bravely take a look at the four horsemen and what John saw and how it lines up to prophecy of this terrible time of suffering and tribulation.

Horseman #1 – The White Horse:

The Rider on the White Horse comes to Conquer. He is the Man of Sin (that old dragon, the devil) who has wished to be worshipped as God, and who declares Himself to be God, and through History has made war with the true and living God, and all of the saints of every age. The rider is the Anti-Christ, and now he takes center stage. He is called, "The Beast," fueled by the Dragon, and aided by the False Prophet. The first order of business for The Beast is to enter a seven-year treaty with Israel. He comes into power through control of the European Common Market. His charm and charisma will be legendary; regardless of how charming and handsome he might appear, this creature will still be the liar that he has always been. A storm of delusion will come upon the world. They will believe his lies, see his miracles, and worship him wholeheartedly.

Scriptures: Revelation 6:2 – The Rider on the White Horse;

Revelation 13:4 – The Beast and who he is;

Mathew 24:21 – The Great Tribulation;

Revelation 5 – The Seven Seal Judgment;

During this period in History, The Beast suffers a mortal wound, and comes to life again, making all those who worship Him, all the more worshipful. He will enter the temple and sit upon the throne of David, desecrating and bringing abomination to the throne. To add insult to injury, he breaks his treaty with Israel after only three and a half years. Israel now enters into what is referred to as, "Jacob's Trouble." They will be hated and hunted down for their very lives. All those that worship The Beast will be branded with his number of 666!

Horseman #2 – The Red Horse (The Color of Blood):

The rider on the Red Horse will be given power to take peace from the earth. There will be havoc, and utter destruction. The Beast's true identity begins to immerge. "And it was given unto him to make war with the saints and to overcome them, and power was given Him over all kindred's and tongues and nations Revelation 13:7. Individuals saved through this period will die for their faith, and it will be a horrible death;

because The Beast will not stand for any opposition. The world will be reeling from the violence, persecution, and strife that are everyday occurrences. The wrath of God will continue to be poured out by God in a way that the world has never witnessed before. Bloodshed will be rampant in that day. This is the day that brother will be against brother, father against son, daughter against mother; husbands and wives will betray one another that will end in death. Blood will flow through the city streets as neighbors kill one another, and racial violence erupts as never before. The sword dripping with blood will precede the stench of decaying flesh. Hatred will inflame the hearts of men; there will be religious and class wars. Weapons of mass destruction will be in abundance. All of the strife and violence will eventually culminate in the final battle of man against man in the Great Battle of Armageddon. Let us come to the realization that man would literally destroy himself in the final battle, if it were not for the intervention of the Son of Man coming in the clouds to end the battle and subdue all of His enemies.

Look at what Jesus says:

"**For there shall be great tribulation, such as was not since the beginning of the world to this time, no nor ever shall be; and except those days should be shortened, there should no flesh be saved, but for the elect's sake those days shall be shortened.**" Matthew 24:21-22.

Let us conclude that hatred turns into bloodshed, bloodshed into murder, and murder ends in death.

Horseman #3 – The Black Horse:

The Rider on the Black Horses brings in worldwide famine. Looking back in history, we can see that after wars have been fought usually hunger follows. This will be the time when crops will be meager. In verse 6 of Revelation 6, John wrote – "I heard a voice in the midst of the four living creatures say, a measure of wheat for a demerits, and three quarts of barley for a demerits."

Man will do a full day of labor for just a loaf of bread. Productivity of food will be at its lowest. Many will die from hunger. Unless one has the mark of The Beast, one cannot receive food or any other services. In this day of great technology the mark of The Beast can be a small computer chip engraved with the numbers 666 and implanted underneath the skin. Once the mark of the Beast is implanted on an individual, that person is doomed for eternal damnation. Those that do not carry the mark will die by execution.

Horseman #4 – The Pale Horse

The Rider on the Pale Horse is Death; coming along with Him is Hades. Hades is the name that refers to the realm of departed spirits. Revelation 6:7,8 aptly describes this ride; Look how John describes this rider: "And I looked, a Pale Horse and His name that sat on Him was Death, and Hades followed with Him, and power given unto them over the fourth part of the earth to kill with the sword and hunger, and with the beast of the earth." This was the most terrifying of the judgments. Death and Hades combined will be given the authority to kill one-fourth of the earth's population, which amounts to nearly one billion people, and they will die by the worst means possible; sword, hunger, and the wild beast that will roam the earth at that time. The unholy spirit world will have a field day; released will be all types of demonic spirits that will torment earth's inhabitants. Viruses and epidemics will be commonplace, without a known cure. Many shall die by this means as well.

Shall we go on? Look at the Fifth Seal. When this seal was opened John reported that he saw "the souls of those who had been slain for the Word of God, and for the testimony which they held; and they cried with a loud voice saying, how long Oh Lord, "holy and true," until You judge and avenge our blood on those who dwell on the earth?" "Then they were given to each of them, and it was said to them that they should rest a little while longer, until both the number of their fellow servants, and their brethren, who would be killed as they were was completed." Revelation 6:9-1.

"I looked when he opened the Sixth Seal, and behold there was a great earth quake and the sun became black as sackcloth of hair, and the moon became like blood, and the stars of heaven fell to the earth, as a fig drops its last fig when it is shaken by a mighty wind Revelation 6:12-13. Already there are signs in the atmosphere to show that these things will take place.

Always it is a privilege to come into the presence of our God. We enter His presence through the avenue of prayer and study of His Word. We need not fear death, when He is our Savior; death is the final step into His presence.

Every Word of God, written in the Holy Bible, will be fulfilled. The King of Kings and Lord of Lord will come one day with the armies of heaven, along with all of His saints. This, His Second Coming, will show Him coming in great splendor and victory. He will sit upon the Throne of David, which is His rightful place, there He will rule the nations with an iron fist, in time he will overcome all of His enemies, including death. That old Dragon, The Beast and The False Prophet, will be thrown into an eternal lake of fire, along with the demonic fallen beings, and all those who chose to reject His offer of salvation from sin. The dead both great and small must appear before the judgment seat of Christ, and the books will be opened, and those whose names are not written in The book of Life, will be separated from God, and The Triumphant Lamb of God; separated eternally by hell's fiery grip.

There are seven judgments coming – "After Death there is Judgment:

1. Judgment of the Believers' Sins at the Cross;
2. Believers' Self-Judgment;

3. Believers' Works;

4. Judgment of Gentile Nations;

5. Judgment of Israel

6. Judgment of Angels;

7. Judgment of the Wicked Dead (Great White Throne).

Believers are called to the Judgment Seat of Christ: They are saved from hell's fire, but their works done in their earthly bodies will be judged. Here Christ will ask all believers what they did with the talents, treasurers and opportunities I gave you? "For we must all appear before the Judgment seat of Christ, that everyone may receive the things done in his body, according to that he hath done, whether it be good or bad

II Corinthians 5:10.

Those who appear at the Great White Thorne judgment are those who refused God's offer of salvation. John wrote: "And I saw the dead, small and great, stand before God, and the books were opened; and another book was opened, which is the book of life, and who ever was not found written in the book of life was cast into the lake of fire Revelation 20:12,15.

After all the plagues, seals, trumpets, and bowls of judgments, The Day of the Lord, The Judgment Seat of Christ and the Great White Throne, defeat of Satan, who will be striped of His power, the Heaven and Earth will be burned up, and a new Heaven and Earth will immerge up from the ashes never to be destroyed again, either by flood or fire, and there the saints of God, will be in heaven with the Light of the Eternal City, Jesus Christ the Lamb of God,-"Let the Church say Amen!"

> "Now I saw a new heaven and a new earth, for the first heaven, and the first earth, had passed away, and there was no more sea, Then I John, saw the Holy City, New Jerusalem, coming down out of heaven from God, prepared as a bride adjourned for her husband. Revelation 21:1,2.

Summary:

Death must come to everyone sooner or later. It comes to everyone born of a woman. There is life after ˙

death. Where you spend eternity depends entirely on you. God sent His son into a fallen world of sin. He was the "perfect lamb," who was sinless and with His blood He paid the ultimate (sacrifice) for sin. Upon Himself, He took the penalty of sin and death for everyone. Through this offer of salvation from sin and death, He offers life now and for eternity. One day He promises to come again (rapture) for all those who have received the gift of salvation. For those who have not a judgment called the wrath of God will fall upon all those who refuse so great a offer (salvation from death into life). Those who do reject this offer of grace, must pay the penalty of their own sins. After the imminent rapture of the church, comes the Great Tribulation, where the Man of Sin is revealed (Satan). After breaking the treaty with Israel, The Beast begins his reign of terror; terror such as the world has never known, nor will ever know again. Judgment will be worldwide. Two witnesses will witness to all those who have not heard the gospel, a 144,000 will also bear witness to the inhabitants of the earth. God will allow this final witness of grace and mercy. Sadly some will reject it, as they carry the Mark of The Beast. Others will be saved, persecuted and executed for their faith. Christ will return with His saints and the armies of heaven, He will reign from Jerusalem (The Throne of David) for a thousand years called the Millennium. Satan having been locked up for this thousand-year period, will once again, go forth to fool the nations. Shortly Satan will no longer have the power that was once his, and he (The Dragon), The Beast, and The False Prophet, will be thrown in the lake of fire forever. The books will be opened and those who names are not written in The Book of Life will be cast into outer darkness and bodily picked up by an angel and thrown into the lake of fire forever, alienated and separated from God forever.

An Invitation Too Good To Be Refused: Don't put off accepting Jesus in your heart, if you have not done so. "Now is the day of Salvation." It is so very simple – acknowledge that you are a sinner, tell Him that you know that He came to die for your sins, and you trust Him to take away those sins, and by faith you believe that He died in your place, ask Him to forgive you of your sins, and simply invite Him into your heart.

Once you have done this, He gladly comes into your heart, (The Father, Son and Holy Spirit). You are now a new creature, saved and cleansed by His blood, on your way to Heaven, having been brought from the Kingdom of Darkness to the Kingdom of Life. Upon your death, whether it be by way of the grave, or way of The Rapture, you will enter His presence.

The book of Revelation gives a clear account of the coming judgments: The Seal Judgments (Revelation 6); The Trumpets (Revelation 8-9); and The Bowls (Revelation 15-16).

Whatever the storm you are currently facing, God can and will make His presence known. He is there to comfort, guide, love and intercede on your behalf. There are so many who feel that life is too hard, they have lost hope. God's presence in our life provides the hope that we need to face today and all of our tomorrows. The Son of God went on ahead to prepare a place for all those that have accepted His great offer of salvation. That makes the future look bright, because "where He will be, we will be also." In this we have victory even over death. The grave cannot hold the soul and spirit of the child of God, it moves into the presence of the everlasting Father forever.

Jesus said- **"And Lo I am with you to the end of the age."** "For Christ has not entered the holy places made with hands, which are copies of the true, but into heaven itself, now to appear in the presence of God for us. He then would have had to suffer often since the foundation of the world, but, once at the end of the ages, He has appeared to put away sin by the sacrifice of Himself; and as it is appointed for men to die once, but after this the judgment; so Christ was offered once to bear the sins of many; to those who eagerly wait for Him, He will appear a second time, apart from sin, for salvation. Hebrews 9:24, 26-28.

You can spend eternity away from Him or in His Presence – The Choice Is Yours!

Chapter Five
God's Care

Gracia Burnham has told her story to reporters and audiences across the United States. Her story has been printed in several Christian magazines. She and her husband Martin, were missionaries to the impoverished in the Philippines. They worked in this ministry for seventeen years. A decision to take their children to visit their grandparents, and go on to Dos Palmas with friends to a Resort on the island of Pal Wan near the China sea, proved to be costly. The Burnham's were captured along with others, and taken hostage by the Abu Sayyyaf, a known terrorist group, famous for violent high profile attacks. Thus, began their fourteen-month ordeal. They were being held for ransom. Day, after day, they were marched through the jungle, sometimes they would be weak with hunger, tired, and exhausted from the harsh ordeal. When their plight was learned, their pictures were flashed on televisions around the world. Gracia reported that Martin aged before her eyes, and his once strong, robust appearance, began to waste away. All through the ordeal, she leaned on Martin for strength and courage. Martin was strong in his trust of God's constant care. He pointed out that they had not been beaten or molested, and his trust that God would take care of them was very strong. Eventually, a rescue that went terribly wrong resulted in Gracia, with a bullet to her leg, and Martin dead. Garcia said that Martin never lost hope and he knew that God cared about them; even in the worst of circumstances; God would take care of them.[3]

In scripture the Lord Jesus is depicted as the Good Shepherd. The Shepherd always takes care of His sheep. The role of the Shepherd in History has always been to go and seek those sheep that were lost. The Shepherd would leave the flock to seek the one that

---

[3]   Burnham, Gracia, One Simple Lesson, Guidepost. July, 2003 - page 30

was lost; so great was His care of them. Look at why Jesus calls Himself the Good Shepherd and He cares for His own sheep:

"My sheep hear My voice, and I know them, and they follow Me; and I give them eternal life, and they shall never perish, neither shall anyone snatch them out of My hand, My Father, who has given to Me is greater than all, and no one is able to snatch them out of My Fathers hand; I and My Father are one." John 10:27-30.

The beautiful Psalm that King David penned, Psalm 23, is one that almost everyone knows. This Psalm is such a comfort – hear the words once again:

" The Lord is my shepherd, I shall not want; He makes me to lie down in green pastures, he leads me beside the still waters, He restores my soul: He leads me in the paths of righteousness, for His name's sake – Yea, though I walk through the valley of the shadow of death, I will fear no evil."

Even if a sheep continually strays from the rest of the flock, the Shepherd will break one of the legs of the sheep, for his own protection, hence the Shepherd will have curbed a tendency of the sheep to be hurt by falling into a trap, or fall prey to wild animals that would kill it. What great care the Good Shepherd provides. Basically sheep are dumb animals that don't know what's best for them; that is why sometimes we are referred to as sheep. There are times that we too, do not know what is best for us, consequently, we must have a shepherd to lead us. Here again, the Good Shepherd knows what is best for you and I, and it is evidenced by His kind care. He will never put on us any more than we can bear, and even in the midst of our temptations, He will even make a way of escape. Remember that it is not our battle but His. What Care!

His care is further displayed in all of creation. The heavens reflect His glory, the earth is His, and all that dwell in it. See His care toward you and I. God is eternal, He was in the beginning, and we see this best in the way He ministers to the entire human race. "In the beginning, God created the heavens and the earth; the earth was without form, and void, and darkness was on the face of the deep, and the spirit of God hovered over the face of the waters." Genesis 1:1-2.

Genesis, the book of the beginnings, gives an accurate account of all that God created. In the beginning the Trinity (Father, Son and Holy Spirit) worked as one to bring the world into existence, only a great God of love, who cared so much for us all, could accomplish such a feat. They are there from the beginning. God, the Father, God, the Son, and God, the Holy Spirit. They function as one (often called the three-in-one).

God, the Father, is the greatest of the three; He is the source of all wisdom, knowledge and power. God, the Son, is the Savior of the world, Jesus said that **"He and the Father are one."** Being the Word," He was made flesh and dwelt among us" John 1:1-3; this meant, since He and the Father are one, while on earth, when men looked on Him they saw the Father. The third person of the Trinity is God, the Holy Spirit. He is probably the least understood member of the Trinity. God, we understand because He is the Creator, the Son, we understand because He is the Savior; but the Holy Spirit plays a far more important role than we realize. Initially, He appears after Jesus ascended (returned) to heaven, on the "Day of Pentecost," in the Upper Room; where the disciples that had gathered spoke in unknown tongues, and those that witnessed this event, understood what was being said, each one in his own native tongue. Let us take time for just a moment to present who He really is and how He functions in the life of the believer. Jesus talked about His appearance in Acts 1:4-8. He said: **"For John baptized with water, but you shall be baptized with the Holy Spirit, not many days from now, you shall receive power when the Holy Spirit has come upon you and you shall be My witnesses both in Jerusalem, and in all Judea and Samaria, and even to the remotest part of the earth."** Now they were empowered to preach the Gospel, because the personage of the Holy Spirit now dwelt within. You and I receive this indwelling of the Holy Spirit at the point of our salvation, but for most of us we must learn to utilize this marvelous gift, learning to become dependent on Him, and sensitive to the promptings that He give us.

Often called the "Comforter," He was left here as our helper to enable us to live a victorious life. There are many things that He does for us, so effortlessly, that many times we are not aware of Him working in and through our lives. His jobs are explicit, He is our guide, and He convicts us of sin, He intercedes on our behalf, He guides, and instructs us in righteousness, He illuminates the Word of God, He warns the believer of impending dangers and/or traps that Satan has strategically set for him or her, He directs, He assures, all while working in tandem with the other members of the Trinity. This is all concrete evidence of the Father's great care for us. He equips us to do the work that He has called us to do. Each person is special to God; and loved by Him. God cares what happens to each and everyone. God wants each individual to realize his or her potential. God desires the very best for each life. He loved you and I so much, that while we were still sinners, He asked His Son, who had never sinned, to die in our place – that's how great His love and care is for us all. How can we escape if we "neglect so great a salvation?" God cares for you, He is concerned about how you think and feel. He hurts when you hurt. Your caring Heavenly Father has felt every injustice, pain or sorrow that you have suffered in life. With great care He extends, His mercy and grace, daily to all. Those who do not know Him as Savior, he continually offers His gift of salvation. To those who do know Him as Savior he offers all of great love and mercy to walk through the difficulties of life, with confidence and security.

Look at what Kind David says about our Lord and how He knew us from the beginning of time, even before the world was called into existence.

In Psalm 139:1, King David stated: "Oh Lord, you have searched me and known me, You know my sitting down and my rising up, You understand my thoughts afar off; You comprehended my path and my lying down, and are acquainted with all my ways." Verse 7:"Where can I go from your spirit; or where can I flee from your presence?" Verses 8-10: "If I ascend into heaven, You are there; if I make my bed in hell, behold You are there; Even then Your hand shall lead me, and Your right hand shall lead me." Verses 13-14: "For You formed my inward parts; you covered me in my mother's womb; I will praise you for I am fearfully and wonderfully made."

Each person is valuable to the Almighty God. Why does God care so much for us, and how is He able to provide such care? I believe that the four attributes that are a part of His character allow Him to do this. GOD IS:

>Omniscient – Has all Knowledge;
>
>Omnipresent- Present Everywhere;
>
>Omnipotent - All Powerful;
>
>Sovereign - Lord Over All.

Scripture tells us that Man is regarded highly by God, "for he has been made a little lower than the angels.

For centuries God has shown great care toward His people the Israelites. At best their History has been nothing short of the miraculous.

God has shown such loving care to Israel, even when they rejected Him as their God. One of the reasons that they were "chosen," to be His people, was because God wanted to show other nations, His great care, but the Israelites did not want to be different from the other nations. They wanted to elect their own King, so they rejected God's care and love for them. History bore out that God allowed them to choose the King that they thought they wanted, but it came at a great price.

Because of their rebellion, the consequences of their sins led to their captivity for over seventy years, their temples in ruin, and eventually dispersement into other lands for decades. Many rejected the worship of the true and living God, as they worshiped idols, and the other Gods that their pagan neighbors worshiped. Even though God was heart broken over His people, He did not forget them, and He still showed great love and care on their behalf.

God saw their sinful state, and took pity on them, He sent the Savior of the World through this line of people. He kept all of His promises to their Fathers. He bestowed on them a land, flowing with milk and honey. Because of their rebellion they became nomads for years, and it wasn't until the year, 1948, that Israel became a statehood, a nation united.

One day in the midst of her trouble (through the Great Tribulation) Israel will turn to the Lord her God, never to stray again. Only a remnant of Israel shall be saved.; 144,000 will bear witness to the world at that time, of the salvation offered to the world through the death of the Jewish Messiah.

Make no mistake about it, there are many today who hate the Jews, and want them utterly destroyed and wiped out of existence from the face of the earth. This will never happen, because Israel is the apple of God's eye, and His protection and care will forever be there working on their behalf.

God came to the lost sheep of Israel, and His offer of salvation and eternal life was offered to the Gentiles as well. God has left no one out, His care and mercy has been graciously offered to all, by way of salvation from sin, and eternal life.

Though the coming days will be dark for Israel, and she will be caught in the worst storm that she has ever encountered. God will not let her be defeated, but will rush to her aid to deliver her victoriously from all of her enemies, and from the tyranny of The Beast.

Remember the Good Shepherd and how He had to break the leg of the sheep for his own protection? Once the leg was broken, the straying sheep would stay next to the Good Shepherd not stray any more. The Good Shepherd has come to save the lost sheep of Israel, and they too will never again stray from the Shepherd and His care.

Look at what John reported that Jesus said about being the Good Shepherd:

"I am the Good Shepherd, and I know My sheep, and I am known by My own; as the father knows Me, even so I know the Father, and I lay down My life for the sheep, and other sheep, I have which are not of this fold, them also I must bring, and they will hear My voice, and they will be one flock and one shepherd; therefore My father loves Me because I lay down My life that I may take it again; no one takes it from Me, but I lay it down of Myself; I have power to take it again – this command I have received from My Father." John 10:14-18

"My sheep hear My voice and I know them, and they follow Me; and I give them eternal life, and they shall never perish, neither shall anyone snatch them out of My hands; My Father, who has given them to Me is greater than all, and no one is able to snatch them out of My Father's hand – I and My Father are one." John 10:27-30.

Look at the willingness of the Good Shepherd to give up His life for the sheep, notice He makes it clear that all of His sheep will reside in one fold, under one shepherd – only our great shepherd can render such care!

Summary:

The Lord Jesus depicted as the Good Shepherd, has come to seek and save all those that are lost. He came to His own they received Him not; His offer was extended to all. One day His people the Jews will return to Him. There will only be a remnant of Israel that will be saved. They will be 144,000 strong (of His brethren) who will carry the gospel in those last days of the Tribulation. They shall be among the last witnesses of the freely offered gift of salvation to the human race. There is no better care!

Chapter Six
God Calms The Storm

Today's world is full of turmoil. There is confusion and chaos everywhere. People want peace; some even want it at any cost. Conflicts in the Middle East seem impossible to resolve. We have already established that we live in the days that were predicted so long ago in the Holy Bible.

Simply stated, without Christ in one's life, there is a void or vacuum that screams out to be filled. The, "Man of Peace," the Lord Jesus, can only fill this void in the human life. As members of the family of God, we experience peace in our lives, when our body, soul and spirit rest solely in the care of our Lord. Even in the storms of life, we do not experience calmness until we have fully learned to lean on the one who brings calm to the raging storm.

On His way to the cross, one of the last times Jesus was alone with His disciples, He talked about vineyards. They could relate to this because they knew that the vineyards produced fruit. A vineyard could, according to its crop, either produce good or bad crop dependent upon its growth and harvesting of said fruit.

Jesus said in John 15:1-7: **"I am the true vine, and My Father is the vinedresser; every branch in Me that does not bear fruit He takes away, and every branch that bears fruit, He prunes so that it bears more fruit." "I am the vine, you are the branches he who abides in Me, and I in Him, bears much fruit, for without Me you can do nothing." "If you abide in Me, and My words abide in you, you shall ask what you desire, and it shall be done for you."** The simple task of "abiding," is to trust yourself completely to the care of the "true vine," while He brings Peace and Calm in the midst of the storms! Bruce Wilkinson in his book, "Secrets of The Vine," noted that the disciples needed to have their fears calmed. Jesus was going away from them, and they needed to know that they could still feel

His presence, after His departure, by simply abiding in Him. Vines produce fruit, and Jesus wanted them to know that their lives could produce fruit as well. They needed to know that calmness occurs when they, the branches, abide in the vine. Charles Stanley, in a book that he wrote, encouraging believers to embrace a spirit filled life said, "The vine is Christ, I am the branch, the Holy Spirit is the sap that runs from the vine into the branch; the branch lives, grows, and bears fruit not by struggles and effort, but by simply abiding."[4]

Our abiding produces fruit in our lives by the power of the Holy Spirit. This is God, the Holy Spirit," living His life through us. The calmness that you and I exhibit in the midst of the storm, is a powerful testimony that God's grace is sufficient to bring us through any circumstance or adversity that we may encounter in this life. It is possible to experience Peace and remain calm in the midst of turmoil and confusion in any given situation. It comes from knowing that our Lord is in control of every situation, and that He can bring order to chaotic situations, while keeping our emotions

---

[4] Staley, Charles Dr., The Wonderful Spirit Filled Life – Page 56

in check. Interestingly one of the fruits of the Spirit is Peace. In order to understand a little better about the Fruits of the Spirit, we must first recognize what they are as outlined in scripture.

Paul in his letter to the Galatians has a good handle on this; look at what he said – they were: "the fruit of the Spirit is love, joy, peace, longsuffering, kindness, goodness, faithfulness, gentleness, self-control, against such there is no law." "If we live in the Spirit, let us also walk in the Spirit." Galatians 5:22-23,25.

When we as believers come to our heavenly Father in prayer, asking for more love, patience, and kindness to be more evident in our lives, we are put to the test. For example, in order to be more loving, we must learn to show love to others, even when they are unloving toward us. That's a test! Sometimes God will allow us to come into daily contact with a person or persons who we find it difficult to love, such as a neighbor, employer, spouse, children, parent, etc., and we have to learn to practice Love if we are going to produce a good harvest of fruit in this area. The same can be said if we want Patience; along will come those situations in life, where we must practice patience. It's very difficult to wait for something that you want so very badly to happen. This could be a relationship that you wish to see cultivate into marriage, or a child that you can't seem to have, a house or job that you want so very badly, or some coveted position or political office that you are aspiring to hold. This tries the patience – and for most of us we fall very short in the long-suffering department, when we are forced to wait for something that we desire so very much. Here again, this is a test. My dear friend, once you and I learn to walk in the power of the holy spirit, we shall produce the right type of fruit in our attitudes and behavior. Furthermore, we will not fulfill the lust (bad fruit) of the flesh.

Recently it was reported that off the shores of a beach in the Chicago area, and surrounded by the vast water of Lake Michigan, rip currents were churning underneath the water's surface. It is evident that with just the right temperature of the water combined, with just the right velocity of wind; this could prove to be a deterrent to any swimmer. At first glance the water appears placid, but if a swimmer stays in the water any length of time; a swimmer could be sucked into a watery grave.

There are hurting people that we see everyday, who present a calm façade to the world but they walk around with hurts that are overwhelming to their spirits. Daily, they must contend with feelings of rejection, depression, anger, grief, low self esteem, frustration, abandonment, compulsions, addictions, eating disorders, stress, emotional baggage, and issues from the past that make the heart heavy.

It doesn't matter whether you wear a designer suit, know all the right people, or feel that you were born on the wrong side of the tracks, and carry the burden of being rejected, unloved, an outcast, on the outside looking in; you still need assuagement from the hurt and pain. We all know that it is possible to feel lonely in a room full of people, to feel numbness in your emotions that just won't go away.

The truth of the matter is, that only God has the power to heal hurting people. God sent His son to heal those that were hurting. He did not come to those that were well, but was sent to those in need of a physician. The blood of Jesus flowing straight from Calvary has the power to heal all of our hurts, and remove the pain by the power of His Word.

Let us address some of the hurts that the human heart can suffer; that rob both mind and spirit from the peace of God:

Depression:

Many people in our society today are suffering from depression. The degrees of depression can vary from individual to individual and if not treated can lead to what is termed Clinical Depression. Depression usually occurs when a person becomes discouraged to the point of giving up hope. Difficult circumstances can affect the mind and spirit to the extent, the depressed individual can no longer cope. In scripture King David was depressed, at one point in his life, we see him in Psalm 42, crying out to God for help. David said; "My soul is cast down within me." Others in scripture suffered from the same emotion, and they too, had to look unto God for help.

Anger:

Sexual, emotional, and physical abuse suffered in childhood or even in adulthood can produce such deep-seated anger in an individual, that many years later the anger can surface, and display itself in horrific acts on innocent members of society. We have all heard of cases where another family member has "gone over the edge" and murdered entire families. Both news, and television reports from time to time, keep track of serial killers who vent their anger and frustrations on those around them in unspeakable crimes.

Low Self-Esteem:

We develop our sense of self during childhood. Basically as children, we accept what people say about us. If our self worth has been trampled on either deliberately or carelessly and/or as the results of the thoughtlessness of others, we can eventually develop low self-esteem. Many a child has grown up and carried feelings of low esteem, because they have not been validated, as they should have been. Others have been victimized by harsh, and critical adults, be it a parent or teacher. It has crushed that person so much that they still feel inadequate, regardless, of how successful they may have become as an adult.

Abandonment:

No one likes to be abandoned. All over the world young children, the elderly, marriage partners, entire families, those in close relationships, can find themselves abandoned by another individual. When this happens, one bear scars of being left behind. We also read in our newspapers and reports, via the Internet, of parents who leave young children to fend for themselves for days on end. This growing problem then becomes the problem of the already over-burdened Department of Children Services in any city or rural locale. Police units are called to pick up day old infants (both dead or alive), from garbage dumps to dark alleys and hallways all over the inner city as well as rural communities.

Guilt:

Women both (young and middle aged), and from all walks of life, have had to deal with the emotional pain of guilt from abortion; although abortions have been legalized, it is still a hot bed of controversy. The shame alone can wreck havoc in the life of a female, who has succumbed to the pressures from both within and without. The pressure has forced her to walk down this path, either by choice or coercion. Many Americans are horrified by the murders of relatives, friends, and the constant barrage of murders printed in our daily newspapers. We are a nation hiding the shame of abortion that is pervasive in every scepter of our society.

Fear:

People are afraid of so many different things. Decades ago, racial minorities feared for their lives. Racial bigotry in our society has been a stench in the nostrils of God for so very long. Wars have been fought because of people's fears; whether it was class, religious, or racially motivated, fear can lead us to act irrationally.

Grief:

Death produces grief; it can be the death of a loved one, or of a relationship. Grief can cause feelings of loneliness, helplessness, fear, and the like. We see that some of the emotions we already targeted can overlap with the emotion of grief. Suicide is rapidly growing in number within our society. Teen suicides have escalated in the last decade. People do not know where to turn for, the help that they need.

Insecurity:

Downsizing in the corporate world has taken its toll on our financial aspirations. Before the days of "downsizing," and scandals like Enron that have rocked the corporate world, many people felt fairly secure with their retirement funds, investment portfolios, and money market funds. People at one time felt fairly safe in their places of employment; but shaky markets, the rise of unemployment, and the rise of homelessness, have left people less secure than ever. Our jobs gives us not only a means of making a living for our families, and ourselves, but also gives stability and meaning to our lives. For many, loss of job means violation of self-worth. The loss of a job can prove to be detrimental to the head of household, whether it is a single parent or a father, strugglings to feed his family.

The Woes of our Society:

We cannot count on the systems of our society to always work for us. Social Service Organizations are limited in what they can provide either financially or emotionally. Our courts are over burdened with the many cases that come before then to be judged. This system does not always work as fairly as it should, and often we witness inequalities in the justice meted out to victims and their families, as well as offenders alike. Crimes of the same magnitude do not always carry the same penalties from state to state, or court to court.

Our political institutions are crumbling. Our churches are failing to meet the spiritual needs of the masses. While our institutions of higher education are graduating students, unprepared to live in today's world. Not everything in our society is out of control, but we are on the path to destruction, if something or someone doesn't turn us around.

Meet The Prince of Peace:

Jesus said in the gospel of John: **"In Me you may have peace, In the world you will have tribulation, but be of good cheer, I have overcome the world."** John 16:33

People who don't have the peace of God in their lives fall prey to some of those emotions that we have just listed. Believers reformed by the Power of God, and delivered from brokenness, can reach out to others who are suffering from the same problems, that they themselves once suffered and can point them to a savior who can heal the hurts and pains of life, and bring calm to the storm.

Time or space does not allow me to address all the hurts of life, or focus on the onslaught of ills that can manifest themselves within the human spirit. Everyday we all rub shoulders with people who need the help of God. People can help hurting people. A reformed alcoholic can reach out and help another alcoholic; a reformed prostitute can help a prostitute, all because they understand their pain, because they have been there themselves.

There is a wonderful book on the market called "God's Power To Help Hurting People." This book gives case scenarios with some of the hurts that people must endure, plus gives scripture verifying others who have dealt in the Bible with some of the same emotional hurts that people suffer with today, along with a devotional guide to follow.

Talking From The Heart:

Our nation was founded upon Christian principles many decades ago. We have pushed God out of our lives and from the American society. We have pushed Him out of our judicial system, political systems, schools, some of our churches, communities, homes and families. We cry out to Him when we get in trouble or when our lives snow ball out of control, or we find ourselves suddenly facing death.

How long will we break the heart of God? How long will we grieve His Spirit? Our high rate of suicides, abortions, and gross immorality are offensive to our God. Our nation, as well as other nations, has become obsessed with sex. Our movies, televisions, and other modes of entertainment have saturated their mediums with sexual explicit images, pornography, homosexuality, and graphic material straight from the pit of the devil. Even the Internet, which is a remarkable piece of technology, has web sites that encourage pornography and pedophilia. Is it any wonder that our nation is suffering from the corrosion of sin? So many of us are not just sick in body, but in our minds. We were created to bring glory to God and enjoy an intimate fellowship with Him, and to bear witness to others of His saving and keeping power; but we fall so short of doing that. Every nation in History that has gone down the path that we are going fell under the severe judgment of God, and some have ceased to exist. The holy, and righteous God cannot tolerate sin, if He could he would not be God, and true to His Word. God does not lie. Every sin will one day come under judgment. Yet we live like He does not hear, nor care what we do. As though He will look the other way, while we rebel and relish our sins. I cannot say it strongly enough; just because He has not judged some of our sins, it is only because He is merciful, and has extended His grace to us. His Word tells us that all of the secrets that we think are hidden, are not hidden from God, and when the books of Life are opened in the judgment they shall be revealed. "Therefore whatever you have spoken in the dark will be heard in the light, and what you have spoken in the ear in inner rooms will be proclaimed on the housetops." Luke 12:3. This verse indicates that some secrets will be revealed even before this life is over. As a nation we need to fall on our faces before God in weeping and begging God for forgiveness of our sins. Yes under judgment all the nations will be judged, however before we are judged collectively, we must repent as individuals. After death there is the judgment.

In this life we have choices; either you pay the penalty of sin, and find that you are separated from God, because you refused to accept His offer of salvation from sin, or you may choose to receive salvation from sin and death, thus one day reigning with Him forever in victory. "There is therefore now no condemnation to those who do not walk according to the flesh, but according to the Spirit." Romans 8:1.

For those of us whose sins have been forgiven and washed in the blood of the Lamb, will suffer persecutions, fiery trials, heartaches and difficulties: James told his Christian brethren; "My brethren, count it all joy when you fall into various trials, knowing that the testing of your faith produces patience. James 1:1-2. Also we read; "For we know that all things work together for good to those who love God, to those who are called according to His purpose." This means that for those who belong to God, even all of the bad things work together with the good things, for our ultimate good, and to bring glory to God. This means that all of the evil devices that Satan planned for you will work out for good, because God will see that it will. All of those things that were hurtful and painful will work out for your good, God will see that it will, and you will be stronger for it.

Students of the Bible, know the story of Joseph. Joseph was one of his father's favorite sons. Joseph had several brothers, and they were jealous of him. Their father showed his favoritism by presenting Joseph with a beautiful coat of many colors. To add insult to injury, Joseph revealed to his brothers that he dreamed that one day they would bow down to him. One day they managed to lure Joseph away from the house, where they beat him, and stripped him of his beautiful coat, and sold him into slavery, to the first folk that came along. He ended up in Egypt. Now God had not forgotten Joseph, and because of the outstanding abilities that God had blessed him with, he soon rose to a prominent position as overseer in the household of the Pharaoh (ruler) of Egypt. Now the story doesn't stop there. The Pharaoh's wife began to lust after him, and she tried relentlessly to entice Joseph to sleep with her, but he would not. One day when she was pursuing him, she grabbed his garment, and he jerked away from her, and fled her presence, with his garment still in her hand. Furious, she told lies to her husband about Joseph, accusing him of rape, and Joseph was thrown in prison. Still God was with Joseph in the midst of his difficult circumstances, and Joseph was given authority over his fellow prisoners. God was in the process of training Joseph for something great. Now God was in the background on behalf of His servant Joseph through the circumstances of Joseph's life. Look what happens next: through a series of incidents the butler and baker of the King was put into the same place where Joseph was. One night the butler had a dream, and God gave Joseph the interpretation of this dream. The dream meant that the butler would be restored into the household of the King, where he could bring the plight of Joseph to the Pharaoh's attention, but the butler forget and Joseph remained in prison for two more years. Now Joseph could have become bitter at this point, and turned his back on God, but he did not. God, still working, caused the Pharaoh to have a dream, and no one was able to give the interpretation of it. You guessed it, Joseph was the only one that could interpret the dream and so the King sent for him; the correct interpretation elevated Joseph to the position of second in command. The dream that the King had was that there would be seven years of plenty and seven years of famine coming upon the land. Now interestingly through the years of drought, Joseph's brothers come to Egypt for food, not recognizing Joseph they bow before him. Eventually he reveals that he is the brother that they sold into slavery, and then they became afraid in revenge he could have them killed, because he was now a powerful man. Joseph is a type of Christ, he forgave them, and said "You meant it unto evil, but God meant it for my good."

This story should encourage believers to continue to trust God through the difficulties that he or she may encounter in this life. God will not forget you in your adversity, but will hang in there with you, providing you with the peace and calm that you need to weather your storms.

Chapter Seven
The Storm Loses Its Intensity

There is one thing that both people and animals alike are afraid of, and that is fire!

Firestorms are very frightening, to say the least. In June 2003, a rash of uncountable fires broke out in various areas of our world. A firecracker in New Mexico ignited one such fire. Raging blazes have been known to destroy quite a bit of property in the forest, and have been a threat to nearby homes. Most of these fires last for days and take a toll on property as well as the human spirit. Eventually the fire loses its intensity due to the saturation of water combined with the force of the human muscle of the firefighters, as they work tirelessly to bring the blaze under control. What a relief it must be to those firefighters, when they see the fire lose its intensity.

When the firestorm moves from the level of great intensity to a lessening of its fierceness, then and only then, can we anticipate the end of the storm! Before we can declare the storm over, our belief system must be in place, that our faith in an eventual end of the storm is forthcoming. Our faith soon will become sight; having said that, our faith must be God centered or we will loose our perspective, and possibly give up before our faith becomes sight. We must run the race (to the storm's end), no matter how arduous it becomes, or long it might take. We can rest assured that our God is faithful! Our faith in Him and His faithfulness to us enables us to comprehend that as the storm losses it's intensity, the end is not far away. Our faith keeps us running the race one step at a time.

One of the greatest runners of his time was Jesse Owens. I had the privilege of attending high school the same time as one of his daughters. When I learned that he was famous, I wanted to know more about his accomplishments.

It was reported that in 1935, fresh from Ohio State University, Jesse Owens tried out for the Olympics and won the "Big Ten Track and Field Championship." That same year, Jesse set world records in four events. They were the 100 and 220 yard dashes; the 200-yard low hurdles; and the long jump. He also made world marks in the 200-meter hurdles

In 1936, further reports showed Jesse winning 100 and 200 meters, in addition to the long jump at the Olympic Trials, qualifying him to go to Berlin, Germany, where he was favored to win all three events.

All of us know, that to become a champion it takes patience, discipline, and commitment in order to obtain the coveted prize at the end of the race. The runner must believe that he or she can make it to the finish line. Faith is often put to the test.

Christians must come to understand, exactly what faith is, and how it will help them run the race, or hang in as the storm moves from intense heat or pressure, into a lessening of the pressure, and finally until when the storm is over and the race has been won.

At this point I wish to examine what Faith is, and how it operates. Once we realize that the storm begins to subside, our faith will continually help us to "hang in there," until the storm is over, and the race has been won! The best definition that I know, has been given in scripture. Turn in your Bible to Hebrews the 11ᵗʰ chapter and look at verse 1: "Now faith is the substance of things hoped for, the evidence of things not seen." The rest of that chapter reads like a – Who's Who, in the Christian annuals of fame, where the victorious saints of old are recorded. One such man was Abraham, who was called to leave his home, knowing not where he was going, to receive an inheritance in a foreign country. He believed in his God to fulfill His promises to make him "a great nation," yet he trusted in God's faithfulness, and this was "accounted to him as righteousness." Does this mean that Abraham never doubted the promises of God, No, there are a couple of recorded incidents where Abraham's faith was shaky, or where he tried to help God out by manipulating circumstances. Abraham grew in the faith, so much so, that one day we see him offering his own son's life on the altar of sacrifice, never doubting that God would spare His son's life by providing the "ram in the bush."

Let us take a little time to look at what happened when Abraham took his son to the top of the mountain because this constitutes a miracle:

"Now it came to pass that God tested Abraham, and said to him, **Abraham!"** and he said, here I am, then God said, **"take now your only son Isaac, whom you love, and go to the land of Moriah, and offer Him then as a burnt offering on one of the mountains of which I shall tell you."** "So Abraham rose early in the morning and saddled his donkey, and took two of his young men with him, and Isaac his son, and he split the wood for the burnt offering, and arose and went to the place of which God had told him." "Then on the third day Abraham lifted his eyes and saw the place far off." "So Abraham said to the young men, stay here with the donkey; the lad and I will go yonder and worship, and we will come back to you." Abraham took the wood of the burnt offering, and laid it on Isaac his son, and he took the fire in his hand, and a knife, and the two of them wept together." "Isaac spoke to Abraham his father, and said my father!" "Then Isaac said, there is the fire and the wood, but where is the lamb for a burnt offering? "Abraham said, my son, God will provide for Himself the lamb for the burnt offering." "Now Abraham and Isaac went to the place that God told them to go, and there on the alter, Abraham laid Isaac bound to the alter, and Abraham stretched out his hand, and took the knife to slay his son (and they both wept)." "The Angel of the Lord, called to Abraham from heaven and said; Abraham, Abraham, and he said here am I!" "Do not lay your hand on the lad, or do anything to him; for now I know that you fear God, since you have not withheld your son, your only son from me." "Then Abraham lifted his eyes and looked, and there behind was a ram caught in a thicket by its horns, so Abraham went and took the ram and offered it up for a burnt offering instead of his son." Genesis 22:1-13.

This is a remarkable story of courage and faith. Abraham had progressed along the road of faith, that he no longer doubted or questioned the Lord his God, nor did he hesitate to do as he was commanded to do, even if it meant killing his only son. Abraham knew that through his seed would come many nations, and even though he had been commanded to do something that made no sense, he knew that the ram in the bush would be provided; because God is always faithful. Our job is to simply trust Him no matter how intense the storm may be, faith will see the intensity of the storm begin to subside, and the battle won!

If you and I can just grasp this concept, we will see many miracles. Oprah Winfrey, in July 2003, presented a program on miracles. One such miracle that caught my attention was the story of Pam Morgan. "One afternoon Pam and her family were traveling back home, after a long trip; all of them were tired. The children were in the back of the vehicle, while Pam and her husband sat in the front, with her husband at the wheel, momentarily, Pam's husband dozed off, and for a split second the family car careened off the highway, and crashed. Everyone seemed all right, but it wasn't long before Pam's husband realized that Pam was not inside the car, but on the side of the road in a crumpled heap, having been ejected from the vehicle. The paramedics rushed to the family's aid, and with the emergency vehicle's sirens screaming, the family's life, and especially Pam's had changed within a split second, as they made their way quickly to the nearest hospital. When Pam arrived at the hospital, the doctors, upon examination of Pam's lifeless form, ascertained that she had sustained a broken neck, and the worst damage, that they had seen to date, to a spinal cord. After surgery, Pam began the long road to recovery. Many people came to encourage her in the weeks that followed, and to continually offer up their prayers. The prognosis looked grim, and doctors were not sure that she would ever recover or return to the quality of life that she once had. Pam in her own words said: "I could not accept a life of sitting in a wheel chair, and I was determined to walk again one day." Day after day, Pam endured, hours of excruciating pain and therapy that would help her once again become mobile. On the day of the presentation of the show on miracles, Pam walked into the studio, unaided, with just a cane to give her support. She credited this miracle to the all-powerful God, and the prayers and encouragement of family and friends. Like Abraham, Pam, and countless others like her, have learned the secret of strong faith, and to never give up on God, no matter the test, or the intensity of the fiery furnace. As you walk on in faith, that hot blast will begin to cool down. Now that was Abraham's and Pam's story, now here is mine:

My Story:

I was born premature. At the time of my birth, infants with low birth weight, were placed in incubators. Little was known of the affect that this would have on an infants' eyes. Studies revealed that with such high levels of radiation, some infants lost their sight, while others were adversely affected. My eyes were affected, and apparently I had suffered some damage to my eyes, which showed up in later life as loss of vision.

In 1964, it was necessary for me to have my retinas reattached. A year or two prior to that, I sustained a serious fall down a flight of steps; which hastened my need to have my retinas reattached. Later, an ophthalmologist told me, that this very well could have happened anyway, due to my earlier exposure to the radiation of the incubator.

Over the years, it became apparent, that my sight was becoming progressively worse. Upon examination, years later, I had developed cataracts, and surgery was necessary. Most patients recover quite well from cataract removal, and are able to function with a great deal of sight renewal. This was not the case with me, as a matter of fact, my sight did well for only about a month or two, however later it was obvious that complications had developed, with eye inflections and blurred vision. I felt frustrated from time to time, by the continual eye exams, eye drops, and living with the uncertainty as to what was happening with my eyesight.

Others were noticing that I was straining to see, and that it was obvious something was definitely wrong with my vision. I was still going to work everyday, and trying to perform my job in the way that I had, when my sight was not as problematic as it had become. My family gave me support, but they didn't realize how limited my sight had become, nor did I want them to worry about me so, I kept my fears to myself. Day by day, I was presenting my problem to my Heavenly Father. The Lord and I had walked together through other storms in my life, and He always saw me through, and had made me strong in the process, so I knew that I could place my faith in Him, through the current storm.

Finally, after one eye examination, my surgeon told me that my sight was not improving, and that I could loose it. That was pretty frightening to hear. A sighted person can panic when told their sight might be leaving them for good.

My Response:

I left the eye center, somewhat in a daze. It was hard to believe that it was that serious. My options were the retina attachments of 1964, could detach through the trauma of the new surgery, resulting in loss of vision; or I could take my courage and faith in hand, and undergo surgery that would be beneficial to my sight. The percentage was lower than I would have liked, for complete success.

The Lord having been with me in all the storms of my life, invited me through His Word and prayer, to continue to trust Him. I didn't receive any great revelation, or hear any loud bells and sirens going off, but with quite certainty and peace, and from past experience, I knew that I could put my faith in Him, to help me retain my sight.

On the day of surgery, I arrived at the hospital, where I would undergo a one-day procedure. I felt at peace. Nurses remarked that I was so calm, and that they wished all of their patients exhibited such calmness. I was told prior to surgery that I would only be mildly sedated, and would basically be awake during the surgery.

On the operating table, I lay waiting for the procedure to begin. During the middle of the procedure, the surgeon stated that it was going quite well.(Victory #1). He also stated that the retina attachment of 1964 was holding quite well in the one eye that was undergoing this procedure (Victory #2). Since I was awake, I could give testimony that I had lots of prayer support behind me, and that the Master Physician was giving him the skill that he needed to operate, and me the faith to believe that it would be successful (Victory #3). Today, I see better than ever, even though I probably will never have what we call 20/20 vision, I rejoice everyday for my sight, and the Lord God's faithfulness to me, taking me through the storm at its most intense heat, to when it began to loose intensity, on to victory at the storm's end.

The Apostle Paul always encouraged the early church to endure their trials; he knew that the removal of the trials would not make them strong, but that endurance would.

His own life bore witness to this. He was ship wrecked, bitten by a snake, beaten, and left for dead; but none of these things, including his imprisonment, deterred him from his faith in God. He counted all of these things as joy, for the Excellency and Knowledge of the Lord Jesus Christ. Down through the ages in the Holy Scriptures, the life and writing of this one apostle is an inspiration to us all. In his own words, Paul said: "imitate me as I imitate Christ." He further encouraged the first century believers to pray not that their trials be removed, but that they learn to endure the trials. He prayed that they become unmovable, unshakeable, always abounding in the truth. He encouraged them never to give up.

The Stresses of Life:

Life sometimes can prove to be highly stressful. We can experience stress from the minute set of circumstances, to the full-blown crisis. Interestingly enough there all kinds of books written on this very subject, in addition to workshops and seminars on "How to deal with stress effectively." I have been privileged to conduct a workshop and speak on learning to deal with stress. In spite of all the self-helps, people still experience undue stress in their personal and private lives. Through trials of lengthy duration, the temptation to give up is sometimes overwhelming, or faint under the trial. The God who loves us will not let us throw in the towel. He holds the reigns of the believer's life, thus inviting us to walk in faith, moving up to higher ground.

It is never easy, but He helps us walk the walk of faith, one step at a time. When our strength gives out, He holds us in His everlasting arms. The beautiful poem, Footprints, gives a clear example of the Savior's love and care as He carries us along in His arms when we feel weak; and in our walk of faith; He carries us along:

Footprints

One day a man had a dream. He dreamed he was walking along the beach with the LORD. Across the sky flashed scenes from His life. For each scene, he noticed two sets of footprints in the sand; one belonged to Him, and the other to the LORD.

When the last scene of His life flashed before Him, he looked back at the footprints in the sand. He noticed that many times along the path of His life, there was only one set of footprints. He also noticed that it happened at the very lowest and saddest times in His life. This really bothered Him, and he questioned the LORD about it. LORD, You said that once I decided to follow you, you'd walk with me all the way. I have noticed that during the most troublesome times in my life, there is only one set of footprints. I don't understand why, when I needed you most you would leave me."

The LORD replied, **"Precious, precious child, I love you, and I would never leave you. During your times of trial and sufferings, when you see only one set of footprints, it was then that I carried you."**

What a wonderful way of expressing our walk, leaning on the Lord in faith, as He carries us on the wings of faith. Yes, life can be harsh, but we must lean on Him, as we traverse our walk through the storm at its fiercest, as it loses intensity, on to when the storm is finally over.

A Return to Faith:

Let us return to the Faith of our Fathers, or to the offer of Salvation by Faith. Let us not be as the Atheist, who says, "that there is no God," or even the Pantheist, that says, "that we are all Gods, God is everything. And God is inside of us all."

Let us be bold in our convictions, and courageous in our faith! Let us press on through the storm until it loses its intensity. As we press on to the end, where Faith finally becomes sight, we will be carried by the one, who has loved us with an everlasting love. Ever dependent on Him that is faithful to see us through from the beginning of life to the end of life. Ever confident "that He which has begun a good work in us, will perform it to the day of Jesus Christ."

Chapter Eight
The Storm Is Over

A church in a small community in East Tennessee was involved in its weekly Sunday evening worship service, when suddenly and without warning a strong wind accompanied by unrelenting rain blew into the area. With a deafening crash and a burst of wind, the church's roof left the building. As the parishioners sat in the darkness and prayed, a small boy frightened by the fierce onslaught of the storm, asked his mother if they were going to die. No, his mother said, "they would be alright." As they gathered outside the church, they all praised and thanked God for their safety, and that the storm was over!

On the cross, the Lord Jesus, hung in pain as He suffered the penalty of sin for us all, Alienated from God His Father, because of our sin, the One who knew no sin, willingly gave up His life. He had completed the mission that the Father had sent Him to do. In a loud voice, He cried out from the cross – **"It Is Finished."** The Storm was over! In just a number of days, He rose from the grave and returned to sit on the right hand of His Father. All of this is indicative of God's great love for sinful humanity.

Who is this powerful entity we call God? In scripture He is introduced as the Creator of all life; He is the God who sees all, He sits on high, and looks low over all the earth; there is nothing hid from Him, even the motives of our hearts. He is called by many names, all translated to mean God. El- designates that He is God. He is El-EloHim, translated to be the Most High God, the sovereign ruler of the universe, the one who is in absolute control of everything and everyone in the vast universe.

Each of His names has a different connotation and application. Let us explore His names:

Jehovah EloHim:

El – means mighty and strong as it refers to God. In the Hebrew EloHim means God. Jehovah is the God who created the universe. He is God, The Father, God, The Son, and God The Holy Spirit, who were in the beginning, and created both heaven and earth. We have looked at how this Trinity works on behalf of the believer, ministering to the believer, in all of the storms of His life. Each member of the Trinity has played a specific role in all of creation. From the beginning. In Genesis 1:26 – God declared **"Let us make man in our image."** Jehovah EloHim, our God is One (The Trinity) functions as one. It is in Genesis that we find man, made in the image of God, and created for God's glory, and to enjoy an intimate relationship with God. He is Jehovah EloHim, the Lord worthy of worship and praise.

Jehovah El Elyon:

Jehovah El Elyon, is the Most High God; sovereign over the entire universe. There is nothing too hard for Him. There is no sorrow too deep, that He cannot heal; there is no valley too wide, that His great love cannot reach across; no tunnel too long, that His love cannot lead us from the darkness into the light. His loving kindness extends from generation to generation, and His kingdom is without end. He is in control of all things, and nothing is impossible with Him. We need not ever fear that the waters will overcome us, or the fiery trial, burn us. Even some of the pagan kings of old, had to pay homage to Jehovah our God as they witnessed His mighty power.

El Roi:

El Roi is the God Who Sees. There is not a heartache that He does not see, nor a sigh that he does not hear. When we feel like a failure He is there to comfort us and pick us up. When we feel rejected, He is there to reassure us of His love for us. He is always aware of our circumstances, and even when we cannot verbalize our feelings, He understands and correctly interprets our groans into utterances, and sees all of our tears, and hears all of our heart's cries and calms all of our fears.

Jehovah Rapha:

He is Jehovah Rapha, The Lord Our Healer. He heals all of our infirmities and diseases. He is the Great Physician, able to heal both body and soul. He comes with healing in His wings. He gave sight to the blind, caused the deaf to hear, the dumb to speak, and even raised the dead during His earthly ministry The Word of God reports that He "came to those who were in need of a doctor, not for those who were well."

El Shaddai:

He is El Shaddai, The All Sufficient One. In the Hebrew Translation Shaddai is equated with. The power of El Shade who pours forth blessings that are both temporal and spiritual. God's love, is a great-unparalleled power to bless His children with blessings. Some of the blessing received is marked through our faith in the hard places of life. God wants us to pass the test that He gives. Unlike the examination that a teacher might give we are allowed to retake God's test, and He will help us pass them, as we learn to lean on Him for strength and His help. God does "great things," for all those who put their trust in Him. When we pass the test that He gives us, we are stronger for it. Coming through the fire we are made stronger by it, and we know without a doubt His sufficiency to carry us through time after time; soon we became to look just like our Savior, as His reflection shines through our lives.

Yahweh:

The Israelites called God, Jehovah. This name was mentioned frequently in the Old Testament. He was their Yahweh, translated, I Am That I Am. The original spelling and pronunciation was so difficult to pronounce and spell that it was shortened to Yahweh.

Moses, standing on holy ground, at the site of the burning bush, inquired of the Lord, whom shall I say sent me to (The children of Israel), **"I Am Who, I Am." "Then you shall say to the children of Israel, I Am, has sent me to you; the Lord God of your fathers, the God of Abraham, the God of Issac, and the God of Jacob, has sent me to you." This is My name forever, and this is My memorial to all generations."** Exodus 3:13-15.

The Great I Am; is He not able to solve any problem that you and I might have? Let us "stand still, and see the salvation of the Lord."

Jehovah Jireh:

Jehovah Jireh, Is The Lord Our Provider. "Our God is able to supply all of our needs according to His riches in glory." Paul understood this truth well; he stated that he knew how to live in Christ Jesus when he had plenty, as well as when he had nothing. Our Jehovah Jireh wants you and I to be able to say the same, and to to be contented whatever state we might find ourselves in. He knows our needs even before we ask Him to supply them; He is capable of meeting our need, even while we are stating it. This goes from the smallest to the largest of needs, from the financial to the insurmountable crisis. The All Sufficient One is just that sufficient in every aspect of our lives.

Jehovah Shalom:

Jehovah Shalom Is Our Peace. "We shall be kept in perfect peace, if our mind stays on Him," who is our peace. Our enemy tries to destroy our peace, for if he can do this; he causes us to doubt God and His promises, as well as destroying our trust in Him who is our peace. You and I, once we accept the Lord Jesus in our hearts as our Savior, become involved in a spiritual battle. Sometimes even the answers to our prayers are delayed, because Satan will do anything in his power to destroy us, our testimony and our intimate fellowship with God our Father. We have to work at maintaining our peace on a daily basis; how do we do this? We can proceed in this area, by daily looking into the Word of God, even when everything around you is in a chaotic state, or you are under persecution of one type or another. Even when you have to war with the doubts of your own mind, our God can give you peace. through the most intense and difficult storm of your life. I can verify this by my own life, when things seemingly were turning upside down in my life, the God of Peace helped me to manifest peace, and joy, that became a witness to those who did not know Him as Savior.

Jehovah Nissi:

Jehovah Nissi is The Lord Our Banner. When I think of the Lord as being our banner, I picture Him riding in with might and power, flag flying in the wind, conquering our enemies and leading us on to victory. There are several accounts in the History of Israel where God came to the defense of His people, in an usual and spectacular way. There will be times when you and I will have our backs to the wall, and seemingly the circumstances that we are facing look hopeless and there just doesn't seem to be any way out. Oh, but when we cry out to the Lord for help, He hears our faintest cry, and comes in with great power and might, making a way where there was no way, or opening a door where there was no door all because He is our Jehovah Nissi. There are some who feel that they don't need God, that they are quite capable of taking care of themselves, and they place their confidence in themselves, their riches, their so called power and might, but oh how wrong they are! These are all things that can fail them, because their trust was not where it should have been – in Jehovah Nissi, the one capable of winning all of our battles with great might and power.

Jehovah Tsebaoth:

Jehovah Tsebaoth is translated to mean The Lord of Host. While we are talking about battles, God is the Captain of the Battle. He is with us in every battle that we have to fight. I don't know about you, but I sometimes feel overwhelmed by the foes I have to face in my own life. I am sure glad that God "has my back," and that I am not in this alone. I have the greatest warrior of them all on my side, which puts me on the winning side. I'm one that likes to see the under dog win, or the home team be victorious.

The Psalmist said "some trust in chariots, others in horses, but we remember the name of the Lord our God." The Mighty Lord of Host has never lost a battle.

Jehovah Tsidqenu:

Jehovah Tsidqenu is The Lord Our Righteousness. God displays His righteousness by His holiness. He invites us to be holy because He is holy. We are to strive to live right in all areas of our lives. We learn to lay aside erroneous thinking as it applies to spiritual truth; we must learn by the power of the Holy Spirit, what is right and what is wrong, that means we must learn to obey God to the letter. We learn by looking into God's word for what is truth, and what is false. God is fair. He is the righteous Judge who will judge the world by His standard of holiness. Everyday someone in this world faces something that is unfair and chips away at his or her dignity. We can always trust God to do what is right or best for us, even when we don't like the outcome, or when it stretches us past our comfort zone. Our Righteous God "works all things together for our good."

Jehovah M'Kaddesh:

Jehovah M'Kaddesh is The Lord Who Sanctifies. Now The Lord Who Sanctifies is the only one who has that distinction of helping us clean the cobwebs out of our lives. We need to walk as believers who are sanctified (set apart) or vessels to be used in ministry to others. We are sanctified that we might live more righteously. This is a process that takes place after our salvation, and will continue on until our day of redemption through to our death. God is patient with us, and He changes us little by little, as we move on from glory to glory in our walk with Him. Initially, after salvation, we are babies in the faith, and must grown toward a spiritual state of maturity. Just as we were babies in our natural state, in order to reach adulthood, we had to move through several states of growth; from infant, to toddler, to adolescent on to the teenage stage and finally we reached the chronological age of adulthood. Sanctification is a life-long process, but in the end we will arrive, and the God who has loved us, will see us through to our journey's end.

God's Character:

God's character is reflected through His many names. We have taken a quick look into what each name means, and it's characteristics. That show how God works, on the behalf of His children, and in the affairs of each of His children's lives. He is our Abba (daddy) Father, delighted when we worship Him, spend time with Him, and call on Him for His help. How can we stay in a state of discouragement and defeat, when we realize that His character depicts that He will be with us in the storms, from the beginning to the end.

There is one book in the Bible where God's name is not mentioned, but His presence felt, that is the book of Esther. Let us follow Queen Esther's story:

Esther:

"Now it came to pass in the days of Ahsuerus, (who reigned over one hundred and twenty seven provinces) in the third year of his reign he made a feast for all his officials, servants, powers of Persia and Mede, as well as all of the powers who were over the provinces before him." Esther 1:1 & 3. At the same time Queen Vashi also made a feast for all of the women in the royal palace, which belonged to King Ahsuerus. (Verse 9). Everyone at both feast were having a great time, and the wine was flowing freely at the feast of the King and his officials. The King surveyed all of his possessions, and one such possession according to him, was his wife Queen Vashi, for she was indeed very beautiful to look at, and he wanted to show her off. Now Queen Vashi was more liberated than King Ahsuerus realized, and she refused to come. Her defiance so infuriated the King that she was banished from the kingdom, and the hunt was on for a new Queen to replace the defiant Vashi. Let us note that even though God's name is not mentioned, He was behind the scenes working things out according to His purposes. Look at what happens next:

In the city of Shusan, there was a Jew by the name of Mordecai, who along with other Jews had been captive in the city for many years. Mordecai had a beautiful niece by the name of Esther. Mordecai had raised her from a young child, since her parents were deceased. When the edict was issued from the King to find a new Queen throughout the land, Mordecai, prompted Esther to apply for the position. God showed His favor upon Esther for she were chosen to be presented to the King, out of all of the other young women for this position. To fast forward in our story, out of all of the young women who came into the King, the King fell in love with her, because he realized that not only was she a virgin, but she asked nothing for herself, and he loved her more than any of the others. Soon the King made a great feast to Esther, and she became his Queen.

Now Mordecai sat in the gate of the king. When the King, and his right hand man, Haman, came through, Mordecai showed obedience to King Ahsuerus, and not to Haman; this made Haman furious, and he plotted to get even. Haman was a proud peacock, who felt that much glory was due him, and it burned him up that Mordecai, a lowly Jew, would not worship Him, as he desired to be worshipped. Soon the wicked Haman devised a plot that would not only destroy Mordecai, but all the Jews as well. What Haman did not know was that Queen Esther was a Jew as well! The plot thickens, as the wicked Haman, whispers into the king's ear, that the Jews are not giving the king, the homage due him, so they must be purged from the land, by death. Soon a decree went out, that all those who did not keep the king's laws, primarily the Jews, would have to be put to death, on orders from the king.

When the decree reached the hands of Mordecai, he implored Queen Esther to do something to save herself and her people. Queen Esther knew that she would have to have an audience with the king. This was not possible unless you were summoned by the king, or upon entering the court, he held out the "golden scepter to one, inviting one to come closer, to have his or her wish granted. Mordecai, pointed out to Esther, that she, being a Jew, was in danger as well, and perhaps she, "had come to the kingdom, for such a time as that." Mordecai tore his clothes, a custom of the Jews when they were in deep distress. Queen Esther knew that she had to do something, so she said that she would go into the king uninvited, and if she perished, because he did not extend the golden scepter, then she would perish. Dressed in her most beautiful attire, she went into the king, and when he saw her, he extended the scepter, and she invited him and Haman to a special dinner at the residence of the queen.

Now Haman, when he found out that he was invited to dine with the king and queen., boasted to all his family and friends, of his great position, and he accumulated wealth. There was only one thing that seemed to elude, him, that his enemy Mordecai did not tremble before him, or give him the honor that was due him. When he complained to his wife about the matter, she came up with the bright idea. A gallows of such a great height should be made and Mordecai should be hanged from it at the suggestion of Human to the king, for his insurrection of the king's laws. Haman felt that this would settle the matter once and for all. So with a glad heart he went to the banquet with the king at the residence of the queen. Meanwhile the king learned that Mordecai had performed a great service for the kingdom and had never been rewarded for it. The king sought to rectify this by bestowing on him great honor in the near future. When the king told Haman that there was a man in the kingdom, who would have great honor bestowed upon him, the proud Haman assumed that he was speaking of him.

When the king, along with Haman, was dinning with Queen Esther, he asked her what her petition was, and she told him that her and her people were soon to be annihilated. The king, furiously replied, "who would do such a thing?' The queen in a clear voice, said this wicked Haman who dines with us. Then Haman became terrified, as the king stormed from the room, and he fell down before Queen Esther, and clung to her clothing, begging for his life. At this time the king returned, and said, "would you force yourself on the queen, in my presence, and he ordered Haman and all of his family put to death on the gallows that he had made for Mordecai. Mordecai received the belated honor due him and he was honored by the king with a royal robe, jewelry, and paraded before the citizens of the kingdom in great honor. The king then sent a decree through out all of his provinces that rescinded his previous decree, and the lives of the Jewish people and their queen was spared. God loves Israel, and a remnant of them will remain forever.

What's In A Name?:

The ancient prophecies of the coming Messiah in the New Testament, verifies His birth and His name. "Behold a virgin shall be with child, and bear a son, and they shall call His name Immanuel, which translated is God with us." Matthew 1:23.

The angel appeared to the Virgin Mary and said: "Rejoice, highly favored one, The Lord is with you, blessed are you among women!" When she saw him she was troubled at his saying, and he said to her; "do not be afraid, for you have found favor with God, and behold you will conceive in your womb and bring forth a son, and His name shall be Jesus, and He will be great, and will be called the Son of the Highest, and the Lord God will give Him the throne of His father David. Luke 1:28-32. Luke further reports that after the child's birth; there was in the same country, shepherds keeping watch over their flocks, and behold an angel of the Lord stood before them, and the glory of the Lord shone around them, and they were greatly afraid; then the angel said to them, "do not be afraid for behold I bring good tidings of great joy, for unto you this day, in the city of David, a child is born, a Savior, who is Christ the Lord. Further, he was called, Wonderful Counselor, Mighty God, Prince of Peace, and Everlasting Father.

His name shall be exalted above all other names, and one day every knee will bow and recognize His lordship and that He was indeed God.

Some today, when referring to God, refer to Him as a "higher power," or "the man upstairs." He is God, able to walk with or carry us through, Until The Storm Is Over!

Chapter Nine
Lessons Learned From The Storm

One event-celebrated worldwide are the Olympics. The first athletic contest was held in 776 B. C. in Olympia located in Western Peloponnesian.

For many, one of the most exciting events of the Olympics is the Opening Ceremony. Each country parades its outstanding athletes with great pomp and ceremony; arrayed with vivid and colorful costumes. The most significant part of the ceremony are the runners handing off the torch, culminated in the lighting of the Olympic Torch.

Each athlete has a story; behind the smiles, are the years of rigorous training. Each individual in order to be able to compete for the coveted Bronze, Silver and

Gold Medals, have learned many lessons along the way.

Both in the natural and spiritual elements, there are lessons that we can learn, that will make us a little wiser and help us to weather future storms. One of the most difficult lessons to learn is self-discipline.

Moses, Joseph, Jacob, and the Apostle Paul, had to learn some lessons the hard way. They learned on the "back side of the desert," or alone in remote places, what it meant to be a servant of Jehovah their God.

In the book of Galatians, Paul so aptly describes what it meant to live under the law. The law preceded the birth and death of the Lord Jesus. The law was a harsh taskmaster. If you broke one law, you were guilty of breaking the entire law. It was impossible for anyone to keep the entire law. The law could point out what was wrong in the life of an individual, but it was incapable of forgiving sins. It was not until the dispensation of grace, were sins forgiven, through the blood of the Lamb of God. Paul made it clear, that some believers were living as though they were still under the law (legalism), with all of its do's and don'ts and harsh punishment. With the forgiveness of sins, no longer is it necessary, to try to live under a rigid, legalistic and stringent set of rules.

Any one in training must not only learn discipline, but endurance as well. Look at the correlation between the two, that Paul addresses in his letter to Timothy:

"You therefore must endure hardship as a good soldier of Jesus Christ; no one engaed in warfare entangles himself with the affairs of this life, that he may please Him who enlist Him as a solider; and also if anyone competes in athletics, he is not crowned unless he competes according to the rules." II Timothy 2: 3-5.

Another difficult lesson to learn is how to walk in love. God extends to us all the agape type of love. God is love and His love is unconditional. His grace that He extends to us is unmerited – we did nothing to earn it, and it is a gift that is free of charge. In the first book of John, written by the same, John describes the love walk that the believer must embark on. "Whoever keeps His (God's) word, truly the love of God is perfected in him, and by this we know that we are in Him." "He who says that he is in the light and hates his brother, is in darkness, he who love his brother abides in the light, and there is no cause for stumbling in Him, but he who hates his brother is in darkness, and walks in darkness and does not know where he is going, because the darkness has blinded his eye." "Do not love the world or the things in the world; if anyone loves the world, the love of the Father is not in Him." I John 1:5,9,10:11 & 15.

John speaks plainly for all to understand, we must not hate our brother because he is of a different ethnic, social status and/or religious background. He who hates his brother stumbles in the darkness. Simply put, within the body of Christ, there should be no divisions, strife or discord. We cannot say that we know Him if we practice sin. John in the sane vein continues- "Little children let no one deceive you, he who practices righteousness is righteousness is righteous, just as He is righteous." He who sins is of the devil, for the devil has sinned from the beginning." I John 3: 7-8a.

Clearly stated, God does not want us to be pretentious in our claims to love others, while at the same time, practicing hypocrisy within our hearts. Scripture ask the question of us: "how can we say that we love God, who we have never seen, and hate our brother who we can see?" We cannot love others, as we should, unless the love of God is within our hearts. A difficult, but beneficial lesson we must learn, if we are to walk, as we should in love.

We must learn to give God praise, and worship Him wholeheartedly as we walk through our difficult storms. Paul and Silas were found singing songs of praise, and giving God, the worship that is due Him, at the midnight hour, after they were beaten and thrown into prison, for the preaching of the gospel. Many of the writers of the Holy Bible were later killed for their faith. They looked not at the present world, but ahead to the glorious world to come.

Lessons must be learned both in patience and long suffering. As we go through our storms, we must learn to be patient with the process and suffer long, until God sees fit to change our circumstances. Change is never easy, and sometimes we long for our difficult circumstances to change to something better, whereas God wants us to change in our circumstances so that we learn to be content in all things. This exhibits godliness, and "godliness with contentment is great gain." These virtues are fruits of the Holy Spirit, operative in our lives. "The fruit of the Spirit is love, joy, peace, longsuffering, kindness, goodness, faithfulness, gentleness and self-control." Galatians 5:22-23.

Hosea: A Man Exhibiting Patience and Long Suffering:

The Lord spoke to Hosea: **"Go take a wife of harlotry, and children of harlotry, for the land has committed great harlotry by departing from the Lord."** Hosea 1:2.

God was making a point in the life of Hosea, by asking Him to marry a harlot. Gomer's adultery, and the children that she conceived that were not Hosea's, was as God felt, when He looked upon Israel's unfaithfulness to Him. Gomer's unfaithfulness and the children that she bore outside her marriage to Hosea, must have torn deeply at Hosea's heart. God is married to His people, and time and time again, they have broken His heart, by clamoring after other gods. In the book of Hosea, the prophet had to buy his wife back, as God has bought His people by offering up the blood of His precious Son. He is pictured as the great Redeemer. God loved Israel while she was yet in her sins, and alienated from Him by her harlotry. His long suffering and patience will one day be rewarded when she turns to Him and recognizes Him as her kinsman-redeemer. Hosea was rewarded for his patience and long suffering, when he was able to buy her back and restore her to the position as his wife. Hosea portrays the heart of God. One day, Israel will be restored to her position. She will recognize Jehovah as her God, she will be brought back to her land, and she will never again be unfaithful to the Lord her God.

God will give His children the needed patience to walk through the storms and will teach the lessons of waiting on Him, until the change comes. Life is unpredictable; it rains on the just as well as the unjust (man or woman who knows God as well as those who don't). We never know what is around the corner, and our lives can change all in a matter of minutes, sometimes never to be the same again.

In August 2004 in the cities along the Northeastern part of the United States, experienced a "Black Out." The power grid short circulated and people living in New York City, Ontario, Canada, Cleveland, Ohio, and Detroit, Michigan, experienced a power outage that lasted for some, more than one day. No one expected this to happen, and people were wondering if it was a terrorist attack. People in New York City felt that it was a flashback to September 11th. Everything came to a screeching halt in people's lives, as many were stuck in elevators, subways, and the like. Many walked for miles in the dark to return home, while others camped out all night on public streets. Others went without food, and one lady went into premature labor on the subway, and finally was rescued and rushed to the hospital. Still others panicked, while others exhibited an air of calm. The point is that since we don't know what's around the corner, at any given moment. Is there any way to be prepared for the unpredictable? Frankly no, there is not; life can some days be a series of irritants that we have to all put up with. It can be a traffic jam, to a long grocery line, to a full- blown crisis, such as a serious car accident, or unexpected explosion at a factory.

Whatever life brings, our lessons are many, from the cradle to the grave, so to speak. God knows the beginning from the end, and He alone, is the only one that can enable us to manifest the "fruits of the spirit," as we learn to appreciate the lessons taught by the Master's hand, as we walk through life's storms.

Chapter Ten
New Life Springs Forth

Have you ever smelled the fresh scent of the grass after a heavy rain? Have you ever noticed how bright the world seems after a heavy rain? Have you ever noticed new life in the budding in the plant life, and fragrance of new flowers in bloom after a storm? All seems right in your world after the storm has passed, as though new life springs forth, a great sense of well being envelopes you in its grasp.

In the book of Ruth, Naomi, Ruth's mother-in-law, passed through a series of storms, before they experienced new life growth. Here is their story:

The Story of Ruth:

The Bible tells us in the Book of Ruth, that there was a man by the name of Elimmelech, who along with his wife Naomi, and their two sons, Mahlon and Chilion, left the land of Judah, because of the famine in the land and moved to the land of Moah. While there in Moab, Mahlon and Chilion took for themselves from Moah, two women as brides. One of the names of these women was Oprah and the other was called Ruth. While in Moah, all three men died, and Naomi and her daughter in-laws were left alone. In her grief and despair, Naomi made the decision to return to her homeland. Having made this decision, Naomi urged her daughter in-laws to return to their own people. After much persuasion Oprah, did so, but Ruth refused. It was so for Ruth to accompany her mother in-law back to Bethlehem of Judah, because she loved her, it was appropriate, to offer her care, so that Naomi would not have to make the difficult journey alone. Ruth in her kindness said to Naomi: "entreat me not to leave you, or to turn back from following you, for wherever you go I will go, and wherever you lodge, I will lodge, your people shall be my people, and your God, my God, where you die, I will die, and there will I be buried., the Lord do so to me, and more also, if anything but death parts you and me." Ruth 1:16-17.

What unselfish devotion, Ruth no longer had any obligation to Naomi, so her motives were purely unselfish, and spoke volumes of the love, that she had for Naomi.

The story tells us when they reached their destination it was in the middle of barley season. Now there was a man named Boaz, who was very wealthy. He was of the family of Elimelech, a kinsman whom others knew for his kindness, and who had many fields where workers gleaned the barley for sale. At the urging of Naomi, Ruth went to Boaz for work in his fields. Ruth needed the income in order to take care of the financial needs of herself and Naomi. Word from others about Ruth, and the kindness that she had shown towards Naomi, had reached the ears of Boaz. Boaz instructed the young men in his employment to not molest Ruth in any way, for she was beautiful to look upon, and let her glean as much wheat as she needed. When Naomi saw that Ruth, was under the protection of her kinsman, Boaz, she recognized and thanked God for moving in their circumstances to bring the help that was needed for their survival, and that her God was looking after her affairs. Naomi further instructed Ruth to seek the security that was needed as protection, and she advised Ruth to go to Boaz in the evening, after he had eaten his evening's meal, and drank and replenished himself from the strenuous day's activities, lie at his feet until midnight and discuss her situation with him, and to seek his advice. Naomi was quick to caution Ruth that she need only to stay until the midnight hour, for propriety's sake. Thus Ruth found favor in the sight of Boaz. He recognized her gentleness of spirit and goodness of heart, and sent by her additional measures of barley, and began to act as Naomi's next of kin, when another closer to her kinship, did not act on her regarding land that would be beneficial for both Ruth and Naomi.

Now it was the custom of that day, for the nearest kinsman, acting on behalf of an elderly female relative, to purchase land for that relative, thus earning him the title of Kinsman Redeemer. Boaz went up to the gate where the elders of the city handled all business matters, and he purchased the land for Naomi and Ruth, that would benefit Naomi in her old age. According to custom he sealed the transaction with the removal of his sandal, thus the land that was given to the deceased males of Naomi's family came to her in a righteous way, all engineered under the protective hand of God, her highest Kinsman Redeemer. God through His son has offered up for you and me His precious blood, thus becoming our kinsman redeemer. Praise God! Now Boaz and Ruth expressed their high regard and love for one another. Ruth the Moabite became the wife of Boaz, and her kindness and willingness to leave her own people, to go to a land that she knew not of, with her mother in-law, returned to her one hundred fold. It was through this earthly line, that the Son of God, Jesus Christ was born. New life comes forth to all with the offer of salvation to all men, through the birth, death and resurrection of Jesus Christ, our Lord!

A New Creation:

When we come to faith by way of salvation in Jesus Christ, we experience a re-birth, "Therefore, if anyone is in Christ, he is a new creation; old things have passed away, behold all things have become new." II Corinthians 5:17. In other words, those old fleshly desires and cravings that we once succumbed to are no longer a part of us. The things that we used to do, we no longer do. The way we use to think, we no longer think. The places that we use to go, we no longer go. We now have new life, and the life that we now have is "hid in Christ Jesus our Lord." We no longer operate under the law of sin and death; this makes us new creatures operating under the principles of new life.

Under the authorship of Moses, in the book of Genesis, we see the formation of new life as it was from the beginning: "In the beginning God created the heaven and the earth." "The earth was without form, and void, and darkness was set on the face of the deep, and the spirit of God was hovering over the face of the waters." "Then God said, **"Let there be light;** and there was light. God made the light day, and the darkness He called night. God divided the firmament from the rest of the waters, and the firmament was called heaven. God made the earth brought forth plants, trees and the grass. He separated the morning from the evening, he brought forth the seasons, days and years, created the stars and planets in their orbits; all of this seemed good to God. God continued on with His plans of creation, He created every living thing that moves from the cattle in the field, to the fowl in the air; again it was all good to God. Then God said **"Let Us (God,**

Father, Son and Holy Spirit), make man in Our image, according to Our likeness; may man have dominion over the fish of the sea, over the birds of the air, and over the cattle over all the earth, and over every creeping thing that creeps on the earth." "So God created man in His own image, in the image of God, He created them male and female." "Then God blessed them, and God said to them; **"Be fruitful and multiply, fill the earth and subdue it, have dominion over the fish of the sea, over the birds of the air, and over every living thing that moves on the earth."** Genesis 1:1-28.

In Genesis, the book of the beginnings, we see that, God created man. He did not evolve from any other life form. Recently, geologist have discovered, that man existed at the same time as dinosaurs, which is another piece of evidence, shooting holes in the theory of evolution.

Pain Brings Great Gain:

New life in Christ Jesus enables the Christian to endure the suffering and/or storms of this present life, as well as the many temptations that we shall encounter along the way. Suffering, in itself, is beneficial to no one. However, it becomes beneficial to us when we enter intimate fellowship with the one who has suffered the most, our precious Lord Jesus. Our temptations and suffering brings forth new life within our spirits, and like the Psalmist, we can say: "It was good that I was afflicted; before I was afflicted, I went astray, but now I keep your word." Psalm 119-67.

Paul wanted to know his Lord intimately, and he realized that this could only be accomplished through suffering. He declares: "that I may know Him and the power of His resurrection, and the fellowship of His sufferings, being conformed to His death." Philippians 3:10. To the Romans he said: "I consider the sufferings of this present time are not worthy to be compared with the glory which shall be revealed to us." Romans 8:18. Paul spoke of his own suffering, which proved to be a thorn in his flesh: "I pleaded with the Lord three times (to remove the thorn), and He said to me, **"My grace is sufficient for you, My strength is made perfect in weakness."** "Therefore, most gladly I will rather boast in my infirmities, that the power of Christ may rest upon me." II Corinthians 12:8-9. Paul encouraged the believers in all those letters and epistles, that they would receive a reward one day in the heavenly places prepared for them by their Heavenly Father.

I must admit that I find it hard to suffer. Our human flesh cries out when pressure is exerted against it. We must die daily to the flesh, and most of us find that extremely painful. As we submit to the suffering or broken process that we must all go through as believers, we are being not only trained by the suffering, but we are being sanctified and purified by the process. Again, Paul encouraged the Roman's: "I beseech you therefore, brethren, by the mercies of God, that you present your bodies a living sacrifice, holy, acceptable to God, which is your reasonable service; and do not be conformed to this world, but be transformed by the renewing of your mind, that you may prove what is that good and acceptable and perfect will of God." The key is that not only do we need to present our bodies, our will, our intellect to God, our minds must be renewed daily. The hardships that we endure are minor, compared to the glory that shall be ours one day. Daily, you and I, are faced with temptations. Temptations can range from immorality, to cheating on our income tax. In themselves, temptations are not sins, its when we yield to the temptation that it becomes sin. Jesus was tempted in all points as we are, however, He did not yield. Therefore, our Savior was sinless, and always yielding to His father's will. Satan tried every way he could to tempt Jesus. Had he been successful, Jesus would not have gone to the cross, and our sins would be ours to pay alone. Satan is so clever. When he appeared to Jesus, he presented to Jesus something that wasn't his to give. He told Jesus that if He would only bow down to him, He could have the world that was presented before Him. Jesus did not fall for his lies and tricks. He stated that it was written, that he should not tempt the Lord His God. Satan had no choice but to leave the presence of Jesus, because Jesus quoted the Word of God to him, and he had no defense or a leg to stand on. This is our best defense, when Satan comes calling to us, trying to convince us that we will not make it through whatever present trouble that we are going through, we, too, can quote the Word of God to him, and he will have to leave our presence as well. Our Jehovah Jared has already made provisions for us to be victorious through every storm, temptation and period of suffering that we must go through, The victory has already been assured, before we even encounter the storm. We can, in faith, look toward the finish line of each storm, while we are in the midst thereof. Suffering makes us strong. We learn to exercise our faith muscle. We experience peace and joy. We become more intimate with our Lord. Our characters and lives reflect His glory. We look like His children should look.

There have been many who have suffered and were tempted down through the ages. Initially, they might not have understood why, but they became confident that God always has a purpose, and a plan that shows that He knows what's best for us all.

Joni Erickeson Tada, a victim of a diving accident, learned a lot about suffering and the fruits that it yields. In her booklet, Great Glory through Suffering, she outlines the benefits that derive from suffering. Joni, was paralyzed from the shoulders down, and became a quadriplegic. Joni had a choice to continue to wallow in self-pity and bitterness, or allow the Lord to wrap His arms of love around her, and walk with her through the darkness into the light, and show her that she could enjoy a new type of life in Him. Today, Joni goes all over the world, lecturing and proving that she is a living testimony for the Master, her Lord Jesus. She writes, sings and gives glory to her God. Today she has a ministry called Joni and Friends; all of this came through suffering.

Two other well renown, ladies in History, were called to be chosen vessels, through their suffering. They shared a common affliction, that of blindness. Biographies written by those who knew, them describe their lives, their suffering, and how it was used as a blessing to the entire world.

Helen Kellar:

Helen Kellar suffered a severe fever at nineteen months. The fever left her blind, deaf, and with very little skills of communication. The Lord sent a young woman by the name of Ann Sullivan into her life. It was Ann who laboriously taught Helen the alphabet. In 1964 she graduated from Radcliff College with honors. In later life she became an activist and lecturer, and later became the founder of the American Foundation for the Blind.

Fanny Crosby:

Fanny Crosby was born blind. In her lifetime she became the most prolific hymnist that the world has ever known. To her credit she wrote over 9,000 hymns. She was also a Poetess. At age fifteen she entered The New York Institution of the Blind, and later returned to teach English and History at this same Institution. She was reported to thank God for her affliction, because without it, she felt that she would not have been the proficient writer of songs, that God brought through years of suffering.

Jesus, Son of God:

There was only one sole, solitary figure that suffered the most. He was God, and He did not use His divinity to relieve His suffering. He went to the cross, the cruelest death imaginable, and laid down His life for His friends. In His temptation, He points to Himself, for all those who are tempted, "to make a "way of escape," through Him," when the temptation becomes unbearable.

Expect the Unexpected:

In late August of 2003, citizens in Emporia, Kansas experienced a torrential rain in the late evening hours.

Drivers attempting to cross through cascading waters beating across roadways, and over swollen riverbeds, found themselves in the middle of a flood. Observers watched in horror as several cars were swept into the over flowing river and vanished from sight. A pastor and one of his deacons, returning home from a conference in another state, ran to alert other drivers to turn their vehicles around, and warned them not to attempt crossing the area, where cars ahead of them had disappeared.

Life is unpredictable; it can change within a matter of seconds and never be the same again. This is why we should take it seriously, a good enough reason to put our lives, in the care of the God, who sees the beginning to the end. God has a plan for each life.

God's Marvelous Plan:

It is not God's will that "any should perish, but that all should come to repentance." His offer of salvation has been extended to all who have been born of a woman. His love is so deep that it is difficult to fully comprehend. God's compassion and His great mercy are there with us through all of life's circumstances. "Nothing separates us from His love." God is the sustainer of all life, and life springs forth anew each day under His ever-watchful eye. God understands all of our sighs and groans, He notes our weaknesses, our infirmities and understands our heart's longings. He sent His only Son, to die in our place. He redeemed us back to Himself. When we were dead in our sins, and were His enemies, He loved us as we were. What great love! New every day are His mercies!

He offers to all, His great plan of salvation. If you do not know Him in the pardon of your sins, His plan of salvation is simple. He extends an invitation to you, asking you to acknowledge that you are a sinner, on your way to hell, and that you need His salvation from sin and the pit of hell. He asks if He can come into your heart, and once He has received your permission, He comes in, cleansing you from all sin, and now you are a member of His family, with heaven as your eternal destiny.

Your refusal of His offer, one day will condemn you, and you will find yourself, upon your death, burning in the Lake of Fire, reserved for the devil, and his demons, forever. This is not a fable, but a reality.

We pray, if you do not know Him, and have not accepted His offer of salvation, that you do so, before it is too late. To reiterate, one day the world will go through turmoil of cataclysmic proportions, that has never been experienced before, or will ever be experienced again. "Now is the day of salvation," not next week or even next year, for by then it might be too late. Why put off this offer, when your soul, is the most important part of you, that you possess?

God gives us choices. He could have made us as robots without a will, however, He chose not to do this; but gave to us a free will, so that when we chose Him, it would be of our own volition, and our recognition of His great love for us, on an individual basis.

Truly, the new life in Christ Jesus brings forth new springs of life that are overflowing.

How do you walk through a storm?

The only way to walk through a storm, is to cling to God's unchanging hand!

Bibliography

Chapter 1

A. B. C. Whipple and the Editors of Time Lire Books
Planet Earth, Storm

Chapter 3

Morgan, Robert J. *Can Christianity Be Proven? Beyond Reasonable Doubt*

Chapter 4

Van Impe, Jack and Rexella *Rapture Hope or Hoax?*

Israel My Glory Magazine, *The Friends Of Israel Gospel Ministry July/August 2001*

De Hawn, Richard *Warning: The Horsemen Are Coming*

Rogers, Adrian, *Triumph Of The Lamb Series Love Worth Finding Ministries*

Chapter 5

Eckman, James *Christian Ethics In A Post Modern World*

Burham, Gracia (her story) *Guidepost Magazine July 2003*

Birchett, Colleen *God's Power To Help Hurting People*

Chapter 6

Stanley, Charles *The Wonderful Spirit Filled Life*

Birchett, Collen *God's Power To Help Hurting People*

Chapter 8

Arthur, Kay *Lord I Want To Know You Kay Arthur Ministries*

Meyer, Joyce *The Redemptive Names Of God Joyce Meyer Ministries*

Chapter 10

Tada, Erickeson Joni *Great Glory Through Suffering Joni and Friends Ministry*

About The Author

Cynthia Wester is the wife of Stanley Wester, and they reside in Rockwood, Tennessee. She is the mother of two grown children, Kimberly Riddle and Adam Wester. She is the doting grandmother of two grandsons, and a granddaughter.

Retired from the Roane County Department of Health, Cynthia serves on it's Board of Health. She is a member of the Ladies Retreat Committee of Cedine Bible Ministries in Spring City, Tennessee. She is an active member and teacher in the Little Leaf Baptist Church, Oliver Springs, Tennessee.

No stranger to personal storms, her salvation through faith in Jesus, plus her strong faith in God enable her to share lessons that she has learned from the storms of life.

LaVergne, TN USA
29 March 2010
177456LV00001B/1/A